LATIN PRIMER 1

STUDENT EDITION

LATIN PRIMER SERIES

Latin Primer: Book 1, Martha Wilson
Latin Primer 1: Student Edition
Latin Primer 1: Teacher's Edition
Latin Primer 1: Flashcard Set
Latin Primer 1: Audio Guide CD

Latin Primer: Book 2, Martha Wilson
Latin Primer 2: Student Edition
Latin Primer 2: Teacher's Edition
Latin Primer 2: Flashcard Set
Latin Primer 2: Audio Guide CD

Latin Primer: Book 3, Martha Wilson
Latin Primer 3: Student Edition
Latin Primer 3: Teacher's Edition
Latin Primer 3: Flashcard Set
Latin Primer 3: Audio Guide CD

Published by Canon Press
P.O. Box 8729, Moscow, ID 83843
800.488.2034 | www.canonpress.com

Martha Wilson, *Latin Primer Book I Student Edition*
Copyright © 1992 by Martha Wilson.
Copyright © 2009 by Canon Press.
First Edition 1992, Second Edition 2001, Third Edition 2009
Cover design by Rachel Hoffmann.
Interior layout and design by Phaedrus Media.
Textual additions and edits by Laura Storm.
Printed in the United States of America.

13 14 15 16 17 18   12 11 10 9 8 7 6 5

Library of Congress Cataloging-in-Publication Data

Wilson, Martha.
  Latin primer. Book I / Martha Wilson ; edited by Laura Storm. -- 3rd ed.
    p. cm.
  ISBN-13: 978-1-59128-054-5 (pbk.)
  ISBN-10: 1-59128-054-0 (pbk.)
  1. Latin language--Grammar--Problems, exercises, etc I. Storm, Laura, 1981- II. Title.
  PA2087.5.W493 2008
  478.2'421--dc22
                              2008035214

BOOK 1

Latin
PRIMER

MARTHA WILSON / Edited by LAURA STORM

canonpress
Moscow, Idaho

CONTENTS

Unit 1: Weeks 1–7   2

Unit 2: Weeks 8–14   43

Unit 3: Weeks 15–21   87

Unit 4: Weeks 22–27   127

Appendices   160

INTRODUCTION

You are about to begin learning a language that most children your age do not learn. It is usually surprising to people when they hear that third-graders are learning Latin. Like most of the people you know, I didn't learn Latin in third grade. I began studying it after I had graduated from college and was teaching school.

Let me tell you a little about what you can expect. One of the first things you will learn is a little saying that begins *amō, amās, amat.* When I was just beginning to teach Latin and told my grandmother what I was doing, she said "Oh—*amō, amās, amat.*" She had learned that when she was about fifteen, and this was almost eighty years later and she still remembered it! You will learn a lot of little sayings like that and if you learn them well they will help you greatly as you learn Latin. Maybe you'll be able to tell them to your grandchildren!

One thing that may seem funny is that nobody grows up speaking Latin any more and there is no country in the world where the people speak Latin. If you want to hear English being spoken, you can go to the United States or England; if you want to hear Spanish being spoken, you can go to Spain or Mexico; if you want to hear French you can go to France. But there isn't a country like that for Latin. The people that spoke Latin were the Romans, and the Roman Empire has been gone for a long time. You might wonder why you are learning Latin if that is so. There are a lot of reasons. I will tell you just a few.

I think that all of you have used these words: *animal, library, elevator, commercial,* and *scribble.* Your parents may have used these words: *constellation, coronation,* and *impecunious.* All those words and many, many more come from Latin words. In fact, over half of the words in English come from Latin. So, while you are learning Latin, you will also be learning English. Once you have studied Latin for a while, you will probably be better at learning and remembering hard English words like *impecunious* and *constellation* and *coronation.*

Someday you might want to learn Spanish or French or Italian. That will probably be easy for you because those languages are what became of Latin in different places after the Roman Empire fell apart. Sometimes I call those languages "New Latin" because that's what they are, in a way.

Let me give you another reason. I think Latin will make you smarter! I had gone to school for many years when I began learning Latin, and I had never had to learn as carefully for a school subject. That is one of the reasons I wish that I had learned Latin at your age. I might have become smarter much faster!

Here is one last reason. You might find that Latin is fun. As you learn , it will take some hard work and you will enjoy it in different ways as you get better and better. But I like Latin, and I hope you will, too!

Valete,
Martha Wilson

PRONUNCIATION GUIDE

Vowels:

Vowels in Latin have only two pronunciations, long and short. When speaking, long vowels are held twice as long as short vowels. Long vowels are marked with a "macron" or line over the vowel (e.g., ā). Vowels without a macron are short vowels.

When spelling a word, including the macron is important in order to determine the meaning of the word. (e.g., liber is a noun meaning *book*, and līber is an adjective meaning *free*.)

Long Vowels:

ā   like *a* in *father*: frāter, suprā

ē   like *e* in *obey*: trēs, rēgīna

ī   like *i* in *machine*: mīles, vīta

ō   like *o* in *holy*: sōl, glōria

ū   like *oo* in *rude*: flūmen, lūdus

Short Vowels:

a   like *a* in *idea*: canis, mare

e   like *e* in *bet*: et, terra

i   like *i* in *this*: hic, silva

o   like *o* in *domain*: bonus, nomen

u   like *u* in *put*: sum, sub

Diphthongs:

A combination of two vowel sounds collapsed together into one syllable is a dipthong:

ae	like *ai* in *aisle*	caelum, saepe
au	like *ou* in *house*	laudo, nauta
ei	like *ei* in *reign*	deinde
eu	like *eew* in *eulogy*	Deus
oe	like *oi* in *oil*	moenia, poena
ui	like *ew* in *chewy*	huius, hui

Consonants:

Latin consonants are pronounced with the same sounds with the following exceptions:

c	like *c* in *come*	never soft like *city*, *cinema*, or *peace*
g	like *g* in *go*	never soft like *gem*, *geology*, or *gentle*
v	like *w* in *wow*	never like *Vikings*, *victor*, or *vacation*
s	like *s* in *sissy*	never like *easel*, *weasel*, or *peas*
ch	like *ch* in *chorus*	never like *church*, *chapel*, or *children*
r	is trilled	like a dog snarling, or a machine gun
i	like *y* in *yes*	when used before a vowel at the beginning of a word, between two vowels within a word, otherwise it's usually used as a vowel

UNIT ONE

UNIT 1: GOALS

By the end of Week 7, you should be able to . . .

- Chant from memory the *amō* and *sum* verb chants
- Chant from memory the present, future, and imperfect verb ending chants
- Recognize a first conjugation verb
- Give the meanings for Latin words (e.g., *aqua* means "water")
- Translate simple present, future, and imperfect tense verbs (e.g., *amāmus* means "we love")

WEEK 1

Word List:

NOUNS

1. caput . . . . head

VERBS

3. amō (amāre). . . . . I love

CONJUNCTIONS

2. et . . . . and

Chant:

Amō, *I love*—Present Active
First Conjugation or "ā" Family Verb

	LATIN				ENGLISH	
	SINGULAR	**PLURAL**			**SINGULAR**	**PLURAL**
1ST	amō	amāmus			I love	we love
2ND	amās	amātis			you love	you all love
3RD	amat	amant			he/she/it loves	they love

> ## Quotation:
> *etc., et cetera* — "and the rest"

Weekly Worksheet 1

name:

A. Write the chant for this week in the box (Latin on the left, English translation on the right). The verb *amō* is first conjugation or "ā" family. Once you've completed the chant, then answer the questions about it.

LATIN

ENGLISH

	SINGULAR	PLURAL		SINGULAR	PLURAL
1ST	amō			I love	
2ND					
3RD					

1. In the sentence, "The rabbit loves carrots," which word is the subject? _____

2. Which word is the verb? _____

3. Is *amō* a verb or a noun? _____

4. In the sentence, "The rabbit loves carrots," would you use *amō, amat,* or *amātis*?

_____

B. Translate each word on its line. When you *translate* a word, you give its meaning in English. The one in italics will probably be harder because you'll need to translate it from English into Latin.

1. amō _____   3. *head* _____

2. et _____

C. Fill in these blanks to answer these questions about *derivatives* of this week's words. A *derivative* is an English word that comes from Latin. The English word must have a similar spelling and related meaning to the original Latin word.

1. The English word *amateur* comes from the Latin word _____.

2. An *amateur* does something because he _____ it, rather than for money.

D. Fill in the blanks about the quotation you learned this week.

1. *Etc.* is an abbreviation for _____ which means _____ .

2. What is wrong with saying "and etc."? _____

_____

WEEK 2

Word List:

NOUNS

1. amīcus . . . . friend
2. canis . . . . dog
3. domus . . . . house, home
4. māter . . . . mother
5. pater . . . . father
6. puella . . . . girl
7. puer . . . . boy
8. vir . . . . man

VERBS

9. audiō . . . . I hear
10. cōgitō (cōgitāre) . . . . I think
11. laudō (laudāre) . . . . . I praise
12. sum . . . . I am
13. vīvō . . . . I live

INTERJECTIONS

14. salvē . . . . Good day! (Be well)
15. valē . . . . Goodbye! (Be well)

Chant:

Sum, *I am*— Present Active
Irregular Verb

LATIN

	SINGULAR	PLURAL
1ST	sum	sumus
2ND	es	estis
3RD	est	sunt

ENGLISH

	SINGULAR	PLURAL
1ST	I am	we are
2ND	you are	you all are
3RD	he/she/it is	they are

Quotation:

Cave canem—"Beware of the dog"

Weekly Worksheet 2

name:

A. Conjugate *amō* in the box on the left and translate it in the box on the right. *Amō* is a first conjugation or "ā" family verb.

LATIN

ENGLISH

	SINGULAR	PLURAL		SINGULAR	PLURAL
1ST	amō			I love	
2ND					
3RD					

Answer the following questions:

1. What is the stem of *amō (amāre)?* _____

2. What is the stem of *cōgitō (cōgitāre)?* _____

3. What is the stem of *laudō (laudāre)?* _____

B. Translate these words from this week's Word List. Some will need to be translated from English to Latin. When you *translate* a word you give the meaning.

1. laudō _____

2. domus _____

3. sum _____

4. puella _____

5. valē _____

6. canis _____

7. father _____

8. friend _____

9. vīvō _____

10. cōgitō _____

11. puer _____

12. salvē _____

13. audiō _____

14. mother _____

15. man _____

C. Fill in these blanks telling about derivatives of this week's words.

1. The English word *maternal* comes from the Latin word _____.

2. *Maternal* love is the love of a _____.

3. There is a hymn that begins with these words: "All glory, laud, and honor to Thee, Redeemer,

King." What do you think the word *laud* means? _____

4. Terriers, German shepherds, and collies are all *canines*. This is because they are all

_____.

5. If a noise is *audible*, that means you can _____ it.

6. The English word *domestic* comes from the Latin word _____.

7. *Domestic* chores are jobs you do around the _____.

D. Write and translate the chant for this week. Then answer the questions.

LATIN   ENGLISH

	SINGULAR	PLURAL		SINGULAR	PLURAL
1ST	sum			I am	
2ND					
3RD					

1. Does *sum* conjugate regularly or irregularly? _____

2. Is this a chant of verb endings or of a complete verb? _____

E. Fill in the blanks.

1. Italian, French, Spanish, Portuguese, and Romanian are languages spoken today in different

parts of the world. They are called _____ languages because they come

from the language of the Romans.

2. The language of the Romans was _____.

3. What is the Spanish word for "friend"? _____

F. The quotation for this week is *Cave canem*. Draw a picture using the words in the picture to show your understanding of the quotation.

WEEK 3

Word List:

NOUNS

1. avis . . . . bird
2. caelum . . . . sky
3. Deus . . . . God
4. flūmen . . . . river
5. lūna . . . . moon
6. lux . . . . light
7. mare . . . . sea
8. mons . . . . mountain

9. nihil . . . . nothing
10. sōl . . . . sun
11. stella . . . . star
12. terra . . . . earth, land

VERBS

13. clāmō (clāmāre) . . . . . I shout
14. creō (creāre) . . . . I create
15. dō (dāre) . . . . I give

Chant:

Present Active Verb Endings

LATIN

	SINGULAR	PLURAL
1ST	-ō	-mus
2ND	-s	-tis
3RD	-t	-nt

ENGLISH

	SINGULAR	PLURAL
1ST	I am *verbing*	we are *verbing*
2ND	you are *verbing*	you all are *verbing*
3RD	he/she/it is *verbing*	they are *verbing*

Quotation:

In principio creavit Deus caelum et terram.

"In the beginning God created the heavens and the earth."

Weekly Worksheet 3

name: _____

A. Write in the rest of the verb endings for this week. In the boxes to the right, write in the "person" that goes with each ending. The first one is done for you.

LATIN

ENGLISH

	SINGULAR	PLURAL		SINGULAR	PLURAL
1ST	ō			I	
2ND					
3RD					

B. Underline the endings of the <u>verbs</u> (these are also called *personal endings* because they show the person who is "doing"). Then translate each verb on the corresponding line.

1. amāmus _____

2. dō_____

3. laudās _____

4. cōgitant _____

5. clāmant _____

6. cōgitātis _____

7. creat _____

8. sumus _____

C. Translate the following words from this week's Word List.

1. lux _____

2. luna _____

3. flūmen _____

4. caelum _____

5. clāmō_____

6. avis _____

7. Deus _____

8. nihil _____

9. mons _____

10. creō _____

11. dō _____

12. star _____

13. sea _____   15. earth _____

14. sun _____

D. This week's quotation is taken from the Latin Bible: *In principio creavit Deus caelum et terram.*

    1. Translate this quotation. _____

    2. Which word means "created"? _____

    3. Which word means "heavens"? _____

    4. Which word means "earth"? _____

E. Translate these words from Word Lists 1 and 2.

    1. audiō _____   6. vīvō _____

    2. caput _____   7. domus _____

    3. man _____   8. and _____

    4. puer _____   9. friend _____

    5. puella _____   10. valē _____

F. Give the stem of each of these first conjugation verbs.

    1. amō (amāre) _____

    2. clāmō (clāmāre) _____

    3. cōgitō (cōgitāre) _____

    4. dō (dāre) _____

    5. creō (creāre) _____

    6. laudō (laudāre) _____

WEEK 4

Word List:

NOUNS

1. discipula . . . . student (female)
2. discipulus . . . . student (male)
3. liber . . . . book
4. lūdus . . . . game, school
5. magister . . . . teacher (male)
6. magistra . . . . teacher (female)

ADJECTIVES

7. bonus . . . . good
8. magnus . . . . large
9. parvus . . . . little

VERBS

10. dēmonstrō (dēmonstrāre) . . . I show
11. dīrigō . . . . I direct
12. doceō . . . . I teach
13. labōrō (labōrāre) . . . . I work
14. portō (portāre) . . . . I carry

ADVERBS

15. semper . . . . always

Chant:

Future Active Verb Endings

	LATIN			ENGLISH	
	SINGULAR	**PLURAL**		**SINGULAR**	**PLURAL**
1ST	-bō	-bimus		I will *verb*	we will *verb*
2ND	-bis	-bitis		you will *verb*	you all will *verb*
3RD	-bit	-bunt		he/she/it will *verb*	they will *verb*

Quotation:

semper fidelis—"always faithful"

Weekly Worksheet 4

name:

A. Conjugate the verbs in the boxes on the left and then translate them in boxes to the right. These are all first conjugation verbs.

LATIN   ENGLISH

	SINGULAR	PLURAL		SINGULAR	PLURAL
1ST	portō			I carry	
2ND					
3RD					

	SINGULAR	PLURAL		SINGULAR	PLURAL
1ST	labōrō				
2ND					
3RD					

	SINGULAR	PLURAL		SINGULAR	PLURAL
1ST	dō				
2ND					
3RD					

B. The word *portō* has many derivatives in English. List as many as you can. Think about what they have to do with "carrying." Circle one of them, and on the bottom line tell what it has to do with carrying.

_____

_____

_____

_____

C. Give the stems for the following verbs.

1. dēmonstrō (dēmonstrāre) _____

2. labōrō (labōrāre) _____

3. portō (portāre) _____

4. creō (creāre) _____

5. cōgitō (cōgitāre) _____

D. Fill in the future tense endings. Then conjugate *amō* in the future tense and translate it.

	SINGULAR	PLURAL
1ST	bō	
2ND		
3RD		

LATIN

	SINGULAR	PLURAL
1ST	amābō	
2ND		
3RD		

ENGLISH

	SINGULAR	PLURAL
1ST		
2ND		
3RD		

E. Answer the following questions about this week's quotation.

1. _____ is the motto of the United States Marine Corps.

2. What does it mean?_____

3. Besides having a Latin motto, the Marine Corps has a name that comes from Latin words. *Corps* comes from a word that you will learn next week. What Latin word does *marine* come from?

_____

F. Circle the correct vocabulary word to complete each sentence.

1. "Go fetch!" is a _____ dogs like to play.

    a) liber   b) lūdus   c) labōrō

2. Marc was a fifth grade _____ who wanted to be a veterinarian when he grew up.

    a) discipulus   b) parvus   c) discipula

3. The Tyrannosaurus Rex is a _____ dinosaur with tiny arms.

    a) magister   b) parvus   c) magnus

4. Last week we read a _____ about a rat, a mole, and a crazy toad.

    a) liber   b) bonus   c) lūdus

5. Often, _____ my little sister how to count the money in her

piggy bank.

    a) labōrō   b) dēmonstrō   c) portō

Crossword

Complete the crossword puzzle! Write in the Latin word for each clue.

ACROSS	DOWN
1. I shout	2. I praise
2. light	3. I show
3. I direct	6. moon
4. I love	11. little
5. God	20. I give
6. I work	21. big
7. school, game	22. sea
8. nothing	23. earth, land
9. and	24. I teach
10. girl student	25. I live
11. I carry	26. girl
12. bird	27. star
13. sky	28. sun
14. always	29. mountain
15. I am	30. boy
16. friend	31. river
17. good	32. dog
18. book	33. teacher (man)
19. father	34. game, school

WEEK 5

Word List:

NOUNS

1. bracchium . . . . arm
2. corpus . . . . body
3. crūs . . . . leg
4. manus . . . . hand
5. oculus . . . . eye
6. ōs . . . . mouth
7. pēs . . . . foot

ADJECTIVES

8. malus . . . . bad, evil
9. novus . . . . new

VERBS

10. administrō (administrāre) . . . I help, manage
11. līberō (līberāre) . . . . I set free
12. mūtō (mūtāre) . . . . I change
13. ōrō (ōrāre) . . . . I pray, speak
14. tardō (tardāre) . . . . I delay

PREPOSITIONS

15. in . . . . in, into

Chant:

No new chant this week.

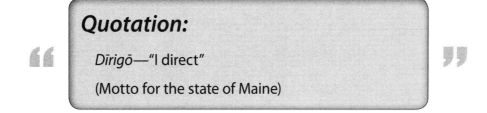

> ## Quotation:
>
> *Dīrigō*—"I direct"
>
> (Motto for the state of Maine)

Weekly Worksheet 5

name:

	LATIN			ENGLISH	
	SINGULAR	**PLURAL**		**SINGULAR**	**PLURAL**
1ST	-ō	-mus		I am *verbing*, I *verb*	we are *verbing*
2ND	-s	-tis		you are *verbing*	you all are *verbing*
3RD	-t	-nt		he/she/it is *verbing*	they are *verbing*

A. Underline the endings on the verbs. Then translate the verbs and state whether they are first, second, or third person. Feel free to use the chart above!

VERB	TRANSLATION	PERSON
administrō	I help, manage	first
ōrat		
līberabit		
tardāmus		
mūtatis		
cōgitat		

B. Fill in the blanks in these sentences about derivatives of this week's words.

1. *Malign, malignant, malevolence, malaria, malady, malpractice, malicious,* and *malice* are just some

of the English words that come from _____.

2. To have *malice* toward someone is to want _____ things to happen to him.

3. *Novice* comes from the Latin word _____ which means _____.

4. If someone is a *novice,* he is a beginner. As a Latin scholar, you are a _____.

5. *Manual* comes from _____.

6. A car with a *manual* transmission is shifted by _____.

7. The word *pedestrian* comes from the Latin word _____.

8. A *pedestrian* is a person who travels on _____.

9. Our English word *oral* comes from the Latin _____.

10. If you are having *oral* surgery, the doctor is operating on your _____.

C. Draw a picture of a person and label these *corpus* parts: *oculus, crūs, pēs, ōs, bracchium,* and *manus.*

D. Give the Latin motto of the state of Maine and its translation.

LATIN _____   TRANSLATION _____

E. Follow the directions given to complete the chants below.

1. Fill in the present tense endings. Then conjugate *amō* in the present tense and translate it.

	SINGULAR	PLURAL
1ST	-ō	
2ND		
3RD		

LATIN

	SINGULAR	PLURAL
1ST	amō	
2ND		
3RD		

ENGLISH

	SINGULAR	PLURAL
1ST	I love	
2ND		
3RD		

2. Fill in the future tense endings. Then conjugate *līberō* in the future tense and translate it.

	SINGULAR	PLURAL
1ST	-bō	
2ND		
3RD		

LATIN

	SINGULAR	PLURAL
1ST	līberābō	
2ND		
3RD		

ENGLISH

	SINGULAR	PLURAL
1ST	I will set free	
2ND		
3RD		

3. Conjugate *sum* in the present tense and translate it.

| | LATIN | | | ENGLISH | |
	SINGULAR	PLURAL		SINGULAR	PLURAL
1ST	sum				
2ND					
3RD					

F. In the blank, give the stem of these first conjugation verbs.

1. ōrō (ōrāre) _____

2. administrō (administrāre) _____

3. tardō (tardāre) _____

4. līberō (līberāre) _____

5. mūtō (mūtāre) _____

WEEK 6

Word List:

NOUNS

1. arbor . . . . tree
2. collis . . . . hill
3. fēmina . . . . woman
4. frāter . . . . brother
5. insula . . . . island
6. nomen . . . . name
7. silva . . . . forest
8. soror . . . . sister

VERBS

9. currō . . . . I run
10. faciō . . . . I make, do
11. scrībō . . . . I write
12. spērō (spērāre) . . . . . I hope
13. vocō (vocāre) . . . . . . I call

PREPOSITIONS

14. sub . . . . below
15. suprā . . . . above

Chant:

Imperfect Active Verb Endings

	LATIN			ENGLISH	
	SINGULAR	PLURAL		SINGULAR	PLURAL
1ST	-bam	-bāmus		I was *verbing*	we were *verbing*
2ND	-bās	-bātis		you were *verbing*	you all were *verbing*
3RD	-bat	-bant		he/she/it was *verbing*	they were *verbing*

Quotation:

Dum spīrō, spērō—"While I breathe, I hope"
(Motto for the state of South Carolina)

Weekly Worksheet 6

name:

A. Conjugate and translate the following verbs. The verbs are all first conjugation or "ā" family.

LATIN   ENGLISH

	SINGULAR	PLURAL		SINGULAR	PLURAL
1ST	spērō				
2ND					
3RD					

	SINGULAR	PLURAL		SINGULAR	PLURAL
1ST	vocō				
2ND					
3RD					

	SINGULAR	PLURAL		SINGULAR	PLURAL
1ST	mūtābō				
2ND					
3RD					

B. Translate the following words. The last four will need to be translated from English into Latin.

1. frāter _____   6. soror _____

2. spērō _____   7. faciō _____

3. collis _____   8. suprā _____

4. scrībō _____   9. insula _____

5. arbor _____   10. woman _____

11. currō _____   13. I call _____

12. name _____   14. forest _____

C. Fill in the imperfect tense endings. Then conjugate *vocō* in the imperfect tense and translate it.

	SINGULAR	PLURAL
1ST	-bam	
2ND		
3RD		

LATIN   ENGLISH

	SINGULAR	PLURAL		SINGULAR	PLURAL
1ST	vocābam				
2ND					
3RD					

D. Fill in the blanks to answer the questions about this week's derivatives.

1. The English word *arboretum* comes from _____ .

2. An *arboretum* is a place which has rare _____ to look at and study.

3. *Submarine* comes from two Latin words and tells us that a *submarine* can travel

_____ the _____

4. *Peninsula* also comes from two Latin words: *paene* which means "almost" and *insula* which

means _____.

5. Therefore, if we combine both words, we know that a *peninsula* is _____.

6. The word *scribble* is a derivative of the Latin word _____.

7. Meaningless or messy _____ is called *scribbling*.

E. Answer the following questions about this week's quotation: *Dum spīrō, spērō.*

1. What is the translation? _____

2. Which state has this as its motto? _____

F. On the lines below, label each picture with the correct Latin word.

| *sōl* | *mons* | *avis* | *arbor* | *canis* | *lūna* |

1. _____

2. _____

3. _____

4. _____

5. _____

6. _____

WEEK 7

Word List:

VERBS

1. cūrō (cūrāre). . . . . I care for
2. dēspērō (dēspērāre). . . . . I despair
3. exspectō (exspectāre) . . . . . . I wait for
4. imperō (imperāre) . . . . I order
5. simulō (simulāre). . . . . I pretend

Chant:

No new chant this week.

Quotation:

No quotation this week.

Weekly Worksheet 7

name:

(Test Practice / Weeks 1-7)

A. Conjugate and translate the following verbs in the present tense.

LATIN   ENGLISH

	SINGULAR	PLURAL		SINGULAR	PLURAL
1ST	cūrō			I care for	
2ND					
3RD					

	SINGULAR	PLURAL		SINGULAR	PLURAL
1ST	imperō				
2ND					
3RD					

B. Translate these verbs from Word Lists 1–7.

1. portātis _____

2. simulat _____

3. imperō _____

4. administrat _____

5. labōrant _____

6. dēspērāmus _____

7. exspectās _____

8. demonstramus _____

C. Translate these words from Word Lists 1–7.

1. amō _____

2. et _____

3. laudō _____

4. liber _____

5. magnus _____

6. ōs _____

7. audiō _____   14. liberō _____

8. domus _____   15. fēmina _____

9. flūmen _____   16. silva _____

10. nihil _____   17. faciō _____

11. exspectō _____   18. dēspērō _____

12. head_____   19. good _____

13. moon_____   20. body _____

D. Give the English meaning for the following Latin quotations.

1. Cave canem _____

2. et cetera_____

3. Dum spīrō, spērō_____

4. Dīrigō_____

5. Semper fidelis _____

6. In principio creavit Deus caelum et terram _____

_____

E. List a derivative for each of the following words:

1. audiō _____   4. māter _____

2. sōl _____   5. terra _____

3. portō _____   6. liber _____

F. Give the stem of each verb.

1. exspectō (exspectāre) _____   2. simulō (simulāre) _____

3. spērō (spērāre) _____   4. cōgitō (cōgitāre) _____

G. Follow the directions given to complete the chants below.

1. Fill in the present tense endings. Then conjugate *laudō* in the present tense and translate it.

	SINGULAR	PLURAL
1ST	-ō	
2ND		
3RD		

LATIN

	SINGULAR	PLURAL
1ST	laudō	
2ND		
3RD		

ENGLISH

	SINGULAR	PLURAL
1ST		
2ND		
3RD		

2. Fill in the future tense endings. Then conjugate *spērō* in the future tense and translate it.

	SINGULAR	PLURAL
1ST	-bō	
2ND		
3RD		

LATIN

	SINGULAR	PLURAL
1ST	spērābō	
2ND		
3RD		

ENGLISH

	SINGULAR	PLURAL
1ST		
2ND		
3RD		

3. Fill in the imperfect tense endings. Then conjugate *amō* in the imperfect tense and translate it.

	SINGULAR	PLURAL
1ST	-bam	
2ND		
3RD		

LATIN

	SINGULAR	PLURAL
1ST	amābam	
2ND		
3RD		

ENGLISH

	SINGULAR	PLURAL
1ST		
2ND		
3RD		

4. Conjugate *sum* in the present tense and translate it.

LATIN

	SINGULAR	PLURAL
1ST	sum	
2ND		
3RD		

ENGLISH

	SINGULAR	PLURAL
1ST		
2ND		
3RD		

2 UNIT TWO

UNIT 2: GOALS

By the end of Week 14, you should be able to . . .

- Chant from memory the *videō* and *possum* verb chants
- Recognize a second conjugation verb and distinguish it from a first conjugation verb
- Chant from memory the perfect and future perfect verb endings
- Chant from memory the first and second noun declensions and decline nouns from both declensions
- Give the meanings for newly learned Latin words
- Translate simple present, future, and imperfect tense sentences (e.g., *Avis volābat* means "The bird was flying")

WEEK 8

Word List:

NOUNS

1. aqua . . . . water
2. diēs . . . . day
3. labor . . . . work, toil
4. nauta . . . . sailor
5. nāvis . . . . ship
6. nox . . . . night
7. patria . . . . native land
8. vesper . . . . evening, evening star

VERBS

9. habeō (habēre) . . . . . I have, hold
10. moveō (movēre) . . . I move

11. nāvigō (nāvigāre) . . . . I sail
12. sedeō (sedēre) . . . . . I sit
13. valeō (valēre) . . . . . . I am well
14. videō (vidēre) . . . . . . I see

ADVERBS

14. saepe . . . . often

PREPOSITIONS

15. ex . . . . out of, from

Chant:

Videō, *I see*— Present Active
Second Conjugation or "ē" Family Verb

LATIN

	SINGULAR	PLURAL
1ST	videō	vidēmus
2ND	vidēs	vidētis
3RD	videt	vident

ENGLISH

	SINGULAR	PLURAL
1ST	I see	we see
2ND	you see	you all see
3RD	he/she/it sees	they see

(Continued on the next page)

Quotation:

ex libris—"from the books"

Weekly Worksheet 8

name:

A. Give the stems of these second conjugation verbs.

1. sedeō (sedēre) _____   4. valeō (valēre) _____

2. habeō (habēre) _____   5. videō (vidēre) _____

3. moveō (movēre) _____

B. Write and translate the chant for this week.

| | LATIN | | | ENGLISH | |
	SINGULAR	PLURAL		SINGULAR	PLURAL
1ST	videō				
2ND					
3RD					

C. In the boxes on the left, conjugate each verb in the present tense. Then translate them in the boxes on the right.

| | LATIN | | | ENGLISH | |
	SINGULAR	PLURAL		SINGULAR	PLURAL
1ST	moveō			I move	
2ND					
3RD					

1ST	sedeō				
2ND					
3RD					

LATIN

	SINGULAR	PLURAL
1ST	valeō	
2ND		
3RD		

ENGLISH

	SINGULAR	PLURAL

Now answer the following questions about the chants above.

1. Verbs that conjugate like *videō* are in the _____ family or _____ conjugation.

2. Which form of *valeō* would you use in the sentence, "The kittens are well"? _____

3. Which form of *moveō* would you use in the sentence, "The snake moves"? _____

4. Which form of *sedeō* would you use in the sentence, "We sit on the bus"? _____

D. Conjugate *nāvigō* in the present tense in the box below, then answer the questions about it. (Hint: Make sure you know what family *nāvigō* is in!)

	SINGULAR	PLURAL
1ST	nāvigō	
2ND		
3RD		

1. *Amō* and *nāvigō* are in the _____ family or _____ conjugation.

2. What does *nāvigātis* mean? _____

E. Give a derivative from memory for each of the following words:

1. patria _____

2. nāvis _____

3. nāvigō _____

4. aqua _____

5. moveō _____

6. nox _____

F. Write two sentences in English. In each sentence, replace two of the words with Latin words from this week. One sentence is given as an example.

1. <u>The *evening star* is shining in the *night.*</u>　　　The *vesper* is shining in the *nox.*

2. _____

3. _____

G. Answer the following questions about this week's quotation.

1. What does *ex libris* mean?　_____

2. Where might you find that phrase used?　_____

H. Translate these words from earlier weeks.

1. māter　_____　　6. cōgitō　_____

2. dō　_____　　7. lux　_____

3. doceō　_____　　8. parvus　_____

4. mūtō　_____　　9. pēs　_____

5. faciō　_____　　10. nomen　_____

WEEK 9

Word List:

NOUNS

1. bellum . . . . war
2. castellum . . . . castle
3. cōpiae . . . . troops
4. equus. . . . . horse
5. gladius . . . . sword
6. ignis. . . . . fire
7. metus. . . . . fear
8. mīles . . . . soldier
9. perīculum . . . . danger

VERBS

10. capiō . . . . I take, capture
11. oppugnō (oppugnāre). . . . I attack
12. possum . . . . I am able
13. terreō (terrēre) . . . . I frighten
14. timeō (timēre). . . . . I fear
15. vincō . . . . I conquer

PREPOSITIONS

16. contrā. . . . . against

Chant:

Possum, *I am able*— Present Active
Irregular Verb

LATIN

	SINGULAR	PLURAL
1ST	possum	possumus
2ND	potes	potestis
3RD	potest	possunt

ENGLISH

	SINGULAR	PLURAL
1ST	I am able	we are able
2ND	you are able	you all are able
3RD	he/she/it is able	they are able

Quotation:

ante bellum—"before the war"

Weekly Worksheet 9

name:

A. Conjugate and translate this second conjugation verb from the "ē" family.

	LATIN			ENGLISH	
	SINGULAR	**PLURAL**		**SINGULAR**	**PLURAL**
1ST	timeō			I fear	
2ND					
3RD					

B. Translate these words from this week's Word List.

1. oppugnō _____

2. metus _____

3. castellum _____

4. fire _____

5. capiō _____

6. perīculum _____

7. contrā _____

8. sword _____

C. Fill in the blank by deciding what Latin word the English word comes from. Then circle the correct definition of the English word by thinking about the Latin word.

1. *Equestrian* comes from _____. In an *equestrian* competition, people would:

    a) shoot with bows and arrows.   b) bake cakes and cookies.   c) ride horses.

2. *Timid* is derived from _____. *Timid* means:

    a) fearful.   b) bold.   c) talkative.

3. *Military* is a derivative of _____. A *military* uniform is worn by a:

    a) nurse.   b) bus driver.   c) soldier.

4. *Terrify* comes from _____. A *terrifying* movie is:

    a) funny.   b) very frightening.   c) sad.

5. *Invincible* is a derivative of _____. If a kingdom is *invincible*, it can't be:

    a) attacked.   b) conquered.   c) seen.

D. Answer the following questions about this week's quotation.

1. Translate the phrase *ante bellum*: _____

2. In the United States, when we use this phrase we mean "before the Civil _____."

E. Write this week's chant in the box and translate it. Then answer the questions about it.

LATIN			ENGLISH	
	SINGULAR	PLURAL	SINGULAR	PLURAL
1ST	possum		I am able	
2ND				
3RD				

1. Do you recognize this pattern from a previous chant? Which one? _____

2. Does *possum* conjugate regularly or irregularly? _____

3. Is this a chant of a complete verb or of verb endings? _____

F. Give the stem of each verb, then write whether it is in the "ā" family (A), "ē" family (E), or is irregular (IRR). Irregular verbs will not have a stem.

1. administrō (administrāre) _____

2. moveō (movēre) _____

3. cūrō (cūrāre) _____

4. possum _____

5. doceō (docēre) _____

6. līberō (līberāre) _____

G. Below, draw all of these things in a picture and label them: *mīles, equus, nauta, castellum, nāvis, arbor, silva, collis, insula, avis, sol, flūmen, mare, mons, domus.*

WEEK 10

Word List:

NOUNS

1. crux . . . . cross
2. familia, -ae. . . . . household
3. fīlia, -ae. . . . . daughter
4. fīlius. . . . . son
5. glōria, -ae . . . . fame, glory
6. homō. . . . . man, human being
7. lex . . . . law
8. rēx. . . . . king
9. vīta, -ae. . . . . life

VERBS

10. agō . . . . I do, act
11. ambulō (ambulāre). . . I walk
12. dēbeō (dēbēre) . . . . . I owe, ought
13. regō . . . . I rule
14. rīdeō (rīdēre). . . . . . I laugh
15. servō (servāre). . . . . I save

ADVERBS

16. nunc. . . . . now

Chant:

First Declension Noun Endings

	LATIN			ENGLISH	
	SINGULAR	PLURAL		SINGULAR	PLURAL
NOMINATIVE	-a	-ae		a, the *noun*	the *nouns*
GENITIVE	-ae	-ārum		of the *noun*, the *noun's*	of the *nouns*, the *nouns'*
DATIVE	-ae	-īs		to, for the *noun*	to, for the *nouns*
ACCUSATIVE	-am	-ās		the *noun*	the *nouns*
ABLATIVE	-ā	-īs		by, with, from the *noun*	by, with, from the *nouns*

(Continued on the next page)

Quotation:

P.S., *post scriptum*—"written afterwards"

Weekly Worksheet 10

name:

A. Complete the chant for this week and answer the questions about it.

	SINGULAR	PLURAL
	-a	
DATIVE		
ACCUSATIVE		
ABLATIVE		

1. Is this a noun ending chant or a verb ending chant? _____

2. Which declension is it? _____

3. What is the gender of most nouns in this declension? _____

Decline *glōria, -ae* in the chart below.

	SINGULAR	PLURAL
NOM.	glōria	
GEN.		
DAT.		
ACC.		
ABL.		

B. Translate the vocabulary from this week's Word List.

1. familia _____   9. fame, glory _____

2. fīlia _____   10. crux _____

3. lex _____   11. rēx _____

4. nunc _____   12. vīta _____

5. servō _____   13. fīlius _____

6. rīdeō _____   14. agō _____

7. homō _____   15. regō _____

8. I owe, ought _____

C. Fill in the name of the conjugation and family of each verb. Then conjugate and translate them.

_____ Conjugation or "_____" Family

LATIN | | ENGLISH | |
SINGULAR	PLURAL	SINGULAR	PLURAL
1ST rīdeō			
2ND			
3RD			

_____ Conjugation or "_____" Family

LATIN | | ENGLISH | |
SINGULAR	PLURAL	SINGULAR	PLURAL
1ST servō			
2ND			
3RD			

D. Underline the endings of these verbs and then translate them.

1. nāvigāmus _____

2. valet _____

3. movent _____

4. timētis _____

5. servat _____

6. sedeō _____

7. habēs _____

8. terrent _____

9. ambulat _____

10. dēbēmus _____

E. Give two derivatives for each of these words.

1. lex _____   _____

2. rēx _____   _____

3. vīta _____   _____

F. Answer the questions about this week's quotation.

1. What does *P.S.* stand for? _____

2. What does it mean in English? _____

WEEK 11

Word List:

NOUNS

1. numerus, -ī . . . . number
2. pecūnia, -ae . . . . money

ADJECTIVES

3. ūnus . . . . one
4. duo . . . . two
5. trēs . . . . three
6. quattuor . . . . four

7. quinque . . . . five
8. sex . . . . six
9. septem . . . . seven
10. octō . . . . eight
11. novem . . . . nine
12. decem . . . . ten
13. centum . . . . one hundred
14. mille . . . . one thousand
15. paucī . . . . few

Chant:

Second Declension Noun Endings

	LATIN			ENGLISH	
	SINGULAR	PLURAL		SINGULAR	PLURAL
NOM.	-us	-ī		a, the *noun*	the *nouns*
GEN.	-ī	-ōrum		of the *noun*, the *noun's*	of the *nouns*, the *nouns'*
DAT.	-ō	-īs		to, for the *noun*	to, for the *nouns*
ACC.	-um	-ōs		the *noun*	the *nouns*
ABL.	-ō	-īs		by, with, from the *noun*	by, with, from the *nouns*

Quotation:

e pluribus unum—"out of many, one" *or* "one out of many"

Weekly Worksheet 11

name:

A. On the following lines, count to ten in Latin.

(1) one   (2) two   (3) three   (4) four   (5) five

_____   _____   _____   _____   _____

(6) six   (7) seven   (8) eight   (9) nine   (10) ten

_____   _____   _____   _____   _____

B. There are many English derivatives of this week's words. Answer these questions about some of them.

1. How many years are there in a *decade*? _____

2. How many years are there in a *millennium*? _____

3. How old is a state when it has a *centennial* celebration? _____

4. How many musicians perform a *duet*? _____

5. How many singers are in a *quartet*? _____

6. How many babies are there when *quintuplets* are born? _____

7. How many sides does an *octagon* have? _____

8. How many couples dance in a *quadrille*? _____

9. In the Roman calendar, *September* was the _____th month of the year.

10. How many horns does a *unicorn* have? _____

11. How many wheels does a *unicycle* have? _____

12. What Latin number do *union, unite,* and *uniform* come from? _____

C. Answer the following questions about this week's quotation.

1. The motto of the United States is *e pluribus unum.* What does that mean? _____

_____

2. Which word means "one"? _____

3. Which word do you think means "many"? _____

4. Which small word means "out of"? _____

5. What is *e* an abbreviation for? (Hint: It's a word you've learned.) _____

D. Complete the chant for this week and answer the questions about it.

	SINGULAR	PLURAL
	-us	
DATIVE		
ACCUSATIVE		
ABLATIVE		

1. Is this a noun ending or a verb ending chant? _____

2. Which declension is it? _____

3. Which gender are most of the nouns in this declension? _____

E. For each noun, write in the blank whether it is in the first declension (1) or second declension (2). The first one is done for you.

1. oculus ___2___   5. lūdus _____

2. patria _____   6. familia _____

3. numerus _____   7. pecūnia _____

4. lūna _____   8. equus _____

WEEK 12

Word List:

NOUNS

1. ager, agrī . . . . field
2. dominus, -ī . . . . lord, master
3. grātiae . . . . thanks
4. mensa, -ae . . . . table
5. porta, -ae . . . . door, gate
6. servus, -ī . . . . slave
7. solum, -ī . . . . floor, ground

ADJECTIVES

8. difficilis . . . . difficult
9. facilis . . . . easy

VERBS

10. audeō (audēre) . . . . . I dare
11. dubitō (dubitāre) . . . . I doubt
12. pōnō . . . . I put, place
13. stō (stāre) . . . . I stand
14. volō (volāre) . . . . . . I fly

PREPOSITIONS

15. ad . . . . to, toward

Chant:

Perfect Active Verb Endings

	LATIN			ENGLISH	
	SINGULAR	PLURAL		SINGULAR	PLURAL
1ST	-ī	-imus		I have *verbed*	we have *verbed*
2ND	-istī	-istis		you have *verbed*	you all have *verbed*
3RD	-it	-ērunt		he/she/it has *verbed*	they have *verbed*

(Continued on the next page)

Quotation:

A.D., *Anno Domini*—"In the year of our Lord"

Weekly Worksheet 12

name:

A. Conjugate and translate each verb in the present tense, and answer the questions about them.

LATIN   ENGLISH

	SINGULAR	PLURAL	SINGULAR	PLURAL
1ST	stō			
2ND				
3RD				

	SINGULAR	PLURAL	SINGULAR	PLURAL
1ST	audeō			
2ND				
3RD				

1. The verb *stō* is in the _____ conjugation or "_____" family.

2. The verb *audeō* is in the _____ conjugation or "_____" family.

B. Underline the ending for each verb and translate it.

1. dubitat _____   4. volant _____

2. servāmus _____   5. timētis _____

3. terrent _____   6. ambulās _____

C. Underline the noun that goes with the verb and then translate the sentences.

NOUN	VERB	TRANSLATION
1. Dominus / Dominī	servat.	_____
2. Servus / Servī	dubitant.	_____

3. Vīta / Vītae   volat.   _____

4. Familia / Familiae   amant.   _____

D. Translate the following Latin sentences to English.

1. Rēx rīdet. _____

2. Mīles audet. _____

3. Avis volat. _____

4. Servus stat. _____

5. Servī stant. _____

E. Fill in the blanks about derivatives of this week's words.

1. *Audacious* comes from the Latin word _____.

2. If someone is audacious, he is very _____.

3. *Facile* is a derivative of _____.

4. A *facile* task is an _____ task.

5. The word *mesa* comes from _____.

6. Why does that make sense? _____

F. Finish this week's chant and answer the questions about it. For the translation, draw a line where the main verb would be. The first one is done for you.

LATIN				ENGLISH		
	SINGULAR	PLURAL			SINGULAR	PLURAL
1ST	-ī				I have ---	
2ND						
3RD						

1. Are these endings for the present, imperfect, or perfect tense? _____

2. Which ending would you use if your sentence subject was "we"? _____

3. Which ending would you use if your sentence subject was "the whale"? _____

G. Answer the following questions about this week's quotation.

1. What does *A.D.* stand for in Latin? _____

2. What is the English translation? _____

H. How many are in each group? Write your answer in Latin in the blank.

1. _____

2. _____

3. _____

4. _____

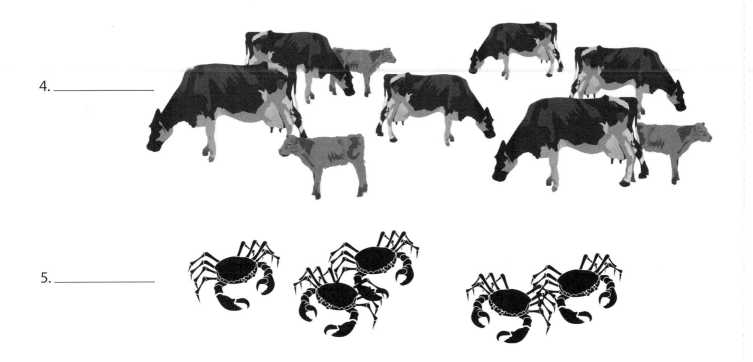

5. _____

I. Decline *porta, -ae.*

	SINGULAR	PLURAL
NOM.		
GEN.		
DAT.		
ACC.		
ABL.		

Quotation:

Gloria in excelsis Deō—"Glory to God in the highest"

Weekly Worksheet 13

name:

A. List the verbs from this week on the blank lines below, and circle the verb in the first conjugation, or "ā" family. Then answer the questions.

1. _____   4. _____

2. _____   5. _____

3. _____

6. The rest of the verbs are all in the _____ conjugation.

7. Another name for these types of verbs is the "_____" family.

B. From memory, translate these words from Latin to English. Most of these words are from previous word lists.

1. digitus _____   7. auris _____

2. capillus _____   8. faciēs _____

3. cor _____   9. corpus _____

4. oculus _____   10. crūs _____

5. pēs _____   11. ōs _____

6. bracchium _____   12. manus _____

The Latin word for "heart" is *cor*, but the French word for it is *coeur*. Use an encyclopedia or the internet to answer the following question.

13. What lake in northern Idaho has the word *coeur* in its name?

_____

C. Translate the following words from English to Latin and circle the verb endings.

1. I obey _____   3. we will watch _____

2. he grieves _____   4. they obey _____

5. mind _____   7. strong _____

6. sweet _____   8. thank you! _____

D. For each sentence, underline the verb ending, then translate it into English.

1. Oculī spectant. _____

2. Fēminae vocābant. _____

3. Cor dolet. _____

4. Equī portant. _____

5. Canis monēbit. _____

E. Write the chant for this week. For the translation, you can leave a line where the main verb would be. The first one is done for you.

LATIN   ENGLISH

	SINGULAR	PLURAL		SINGULAR	PLURAL
1ST	-erō			I will have ---	
2ND					
3RD					

1. Are these endings for the future, perfect, or future perfect tense? _____

2. Does an ending mean anything if it isn't connected to a verb? _____

F. This week's quotation is *Gloria in excelsis Deō*. Answer the following questions about it.

1. What does it mean? _____

_____

2. Who in the Bible first sang this? _____

3. Why did they sing it? _____

G. For each noun, write in the blank whether it is in the first declension (1) or second declension (2).

1. capillus, -ī _____   5. digitus, -ī _____

2. mensa, -ae _____   6. dominus, -ī _____

3. porta, -ae _____   7. vīta, -ae _____

4. servus, -ī _____   8. Deus, -ī _____

H. This is a verse from the Latin Bible. The underlined words should look familiar. See if you can figure out what it says!

Et subito facta est cum angelo multitudo militiae caelestis laudantium Deum et dicentium gloria in altissimis Deo et in terra pax in hominibus bonae voluntatis.

_____

_____

_____

WEEK 14

Word List:

VERBS

1. dēleō (dēlēre) . . . . I destroy
2. fleō (flēre) . . . . I weep
3. necō (necāre) . . . . I kill
4. occupō (occupāre). . . . . . I seize
5. respondeō (respondēre) . . . I answer

Chant:

No new chant this week.

Quotation:

No quotation this week.

Weekly Worksheet 14 *name:*

(Test Practice / Weeks 8-14)

A. For each verb, write in the blank to the left whether it is in the first or second conjugation. Then conjugate it in the present tense.

	SINGULAR	PLURAL
1ST	occupō	
2ND		
3RD		

	SINGULAR	PLURAL
1ST	dēbeō	
2ND		
3RD		

	SINGULAR	PLURAL
1ST	sedeō	
2ND		
3RD		

B. For each verb, underline its ending, then translate it into English.

1. dēbēs _____   3. habēmus _____

2. pāret _____   4. necant _____

5. respondēbātis _____ 9. dolēbō _____

6. audēbunt _____ 10. flēmus _____

7. timēbās _____ 11. rīdēbat _____

8. statīs _____ 12. doceō _____

C. For each noun, write in the blank whether it is in the first declension (1) or second declension (2).

1. dominus _____ 5. puella _____

2. porta _____ 6. capillus _____

3. mensa _____ 7. servus _____

4. digitus _____ 8. terra _____

D. Translate these words from the last seven weeks.

1. patria _____ 9. nāvis _____

2. diēs _____ 10. sailor _____

3. war _____ 11. cōpiae _____

4. vīta _____ 12. nunc _____

5. king _____ 13. mille _____

6. dominus _____ 14. porta _____

7. slave _____ 15. mind _____

8. cor _____ 16. auris _____

E. Use your knowledge of Latin quotations to answer these questions.

1. An *antebellum* mansion was built _____ .

2. *Ex libris John* in a book tells you it is _____ .

3. In Latin, *A.D.* 70 stands for _____ .

4. Translated it means _____ .

5. When you see *P.S.* at the end of a letter, it stands for _____ .

6. When you translate this into English, it means _____ .

7. *E pluribus unum* on a penny is translated _____ .

8. When you sing *Gloria in excelsis Deō*, what are you singing?

_____

F. Draw a line to match each derivative with its Latin root.

1. mental	vīta
2. nautical	spectō
3. nocturnal	mīles
4. vitality	mens
5. spectator	nauta
6. military	nox

G. Count from one to ten in Latin.

(1) one	(2) two	(3) three	(4) four	(5) five
_____	_____	_____	_____	_____

(6) six	(7) seven	(8) eight	(9) nine	(10) ten
_____	_____	_____	_____	_____

H. Underline the noun that goes with the verb and then translate the sentences.

NOUN	VERB	TRANSLATION
1. Dominus / Dominī	dēlectat.	_____
2. Equus / Equī	spectant.	_____
3. Nauta / Nautae	simulant.	_____
4. Puella / Puellae	ambulābat.	_____
5. Servus / Servī	respondēbit.	_____

I. Complete the chants from memory! For *videō,* give the translation. For the other chants, write in the blank whether they are noun ending, verb ending, or verb chants.

LATIN

ENGLISH

	SINGULAR	PLURAL		SINGULAR	PLURAL
1ST	videō				
2ND					
3RD					

	SINGULAR	PLURAL
1ST	possum	
2ND		
3RD		

_____

	SINGULAR	PLURAL
1ST	-ī	
2ND		
3RD		

_____

	SINGULAR	PLURAL
NOM.	-a	
GEN.		
DAT.		
ACC.		
ABL.		

	SINGULAR	PLURAL
NOM.	-us	
GEN.		
DAT.		
ACC.		
ABL.		

	SINGULAR	PLURAL
1ST	-erō	
2ND		
3RD		

3 <u>UNIT THREE</u>

UNIT 3: GOALS

By the end of Week 21, you should be able to . . .

- Chant from memory the pluperfect active verb endings as well as the present, future, and imperfect passive endings
- Give the meanings for newly learned Latin words
- Translate simple sentences involving adverbs (e.g., *Lupus clam occultābat* means "The wolf was hiding secretly")
- Chant from memory the second declension neuter noun endings and decline second declension neuter nouns

WEEK 15

Word List:

NOUNS

1. aedificium . . . . building
2. cīvis . . . . citizen
3. Gallia, -ae . . . . Gaul
4. Germānia, -ae. . . . . Germany
5. Hispānia, -ae . . . . Spain
6. Ītalia, -ae . . . . Italy
7. oppidum . . . . town
8. Rōma, -ae . . . . Rome
9. urbs . . . . city
10. via, -ae . . . . road, way

VERBS

11. augeō (augēre) . . . . I increase
12. commūnicō (commūnicāre) . . . .I share, inform
13. iuvō (iuvāre) . . . . I help
14. maneō (manēre) . . . . I remain
15. mereō (merēre) . . . . I deserve

Chant:

Pluperfect Active Verb Endings

	LATIN			ENGLISH	
	SINGULAR	PLURAL		SINGULAR	PLURAL
1ST	-eram	-erāmus		I had *verbed*	we had *verbed*
2ND	-erās	-eratis		you had *verbed*	you all had *verbed*
3RD	-erat	-erant		he/she/it had *verbed*	they had *verbed*

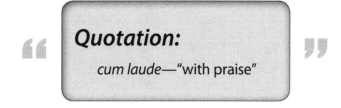

" **Quotation:**

cum laude—"with praise" "

Weekly Worksheet 15

name:

A. Write the chant for this week, and then answer the questions about it. For the translation, you can leave a line where the main verb would be. The first one is done for you.

LATIN

ENGLISH

	SINGULAR	PLURAL		SINGULAR	PLURAL
1ST	-eram			I had ---	
2ND					
3RD					

1. Are these noun endings or verb endings? _____

2. Are these endings for the future, pluperfect, or imperfect tense? _____

3. Which ending would you use in the sentence, "The volcano had erupted"? _____

4. Which ending would you use in the sentence, "You had wondered"? _____

B. List the verbs for this week according to whether they are in the first or second conjugation. You will have some spaces left over in each of the columns. Fill those spaces with verbs you've already learned in each conjugation. (Hint: This week, there are two words in the first conjugation or "ā" family, and three words in the second conjugation or "ē" family.)

FIRST CONJUGATION	SECOND CONJUGATION

C. Conjugate the following verbs in the boxes below and translate them.

LATIN ENGLISH

	SINGULAR	PLURAL	SINGULAR	PLURAL
1ST	iuvō			
2ND				
3RD				

LATIN ENGLISH

	SINGULAR	PLURAL	SINGULAR	PLURAL
1ST	augeō			
2ND				
3RD				

D. The words in italics in the sentences below are derivatives of words from this week. Circle the correct choice based on the Latin words you've learned.

1. *Urban* planning is planning of:

    a) gardens.   b) parties.   c) cities.

2. An *edifice* is a large:

    a) building.   b) forest.   c) arena.

3. If a ship is sailing to New York *via* the Panama Canal, it is:

    a) avoiding the canal.   b) going by way of the canal.   c) not really going.

4. A *permanent* decision is:

    a) very weak.   b) not going to change.   c) quick and easy.

E. Give this week's quotation and its translation.

LATIN _____   TRANSLATION _____

F. Use a map, an encyclopedia, or the internet to find the following places and label them below.

Germānia   Hispānia   Ītalia   Rōma

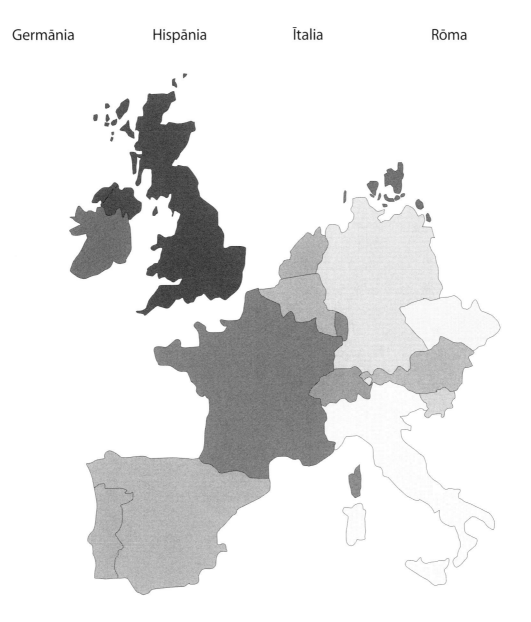

G. Underline the noun that goes with the verb and then translate the sentences.

NOUN	VERB	TRANSLATION
1. Deus / Deī	creat.	_____
2. Magistra / Magistrae	dēmonstrant.	_____
3. Nauta / Nautae	labōrat.	_____
4. Lūdus / Lūdī	mūtat.	_____
5. Fēmina / Fēminae	spērant.	_____
6. Fīlius / Fīliī	oppugnant.	_____
7. Amicus / Amicī	iuvat.	_____
8. Puella / Puellae	tardant.	_____

WEEK 16

Word List:

NOUNS

1. campus, -ī . . . . level area, athletic field
2. captīvus, -ī . . . . . . captive
3. castra . . . . camp
4. moenia . . . . fortifications, city walls
5. mūrus, -ī . . . . wall
6. praeda, -ae . . . . . plunder, booty
7. praefectus, -ī . . . . officer
8. princeps . . . . chief

9. vīcus, -ī . . . . village
10. vulnus . . . . wound

VERBS

11. exerceō (exercēre) . . . . . . I train, exercise
12. parō (parāre) . . . . I prepare
13. putō (putāre) . . . . I think
14. recuperō (recuperāre) . . . . I recover
15. superō (superāre) . . . . . . I conquer

Chant:

Present Passive Verb Endings

	LATIN			ENGLISH	
	SINGULAR	PLURAL		SINGULAR	PLURAL
1ST	-r	-mur		I am being *verbed*	we are being *verbed*
2ND	-ris	-minī		you are being *verbed*	you all are being *verbed*
3RD	-tur	-ntur		he/she/it is being *verbed*	they are being *verbed*

Quotation:

Hannibal ad portas—"Hannibal is at the gates"

Weekly Worksheet 16   *name:* _____

A. Complete this week's chant and answer the questions about it.

	SINGULAR	PLURAL
1ST	-r	
2ND		
3RD		

1. Are these verb endings or noun endings? _____

2. This chant is called the "present _____."

3. In order to have meaning in a sentence, an ending *must* be attached to a _____ .

B. Decline the following nouns and write which declension each one is in. Then answer the questions.

_____ Declension

	SINGULAR	PLURAL
NOM.	mūrus	
GEN.		
DAT.		
ACC.		
ABL.		

_____ Declension

	SINGULAR	PLURAL
NOM.	praeda	
GEN.		
DAT.		
ACC.		
ABL.		

1. Which case is used for subjects? _____

2. Which declension has mostly masculine nouns? _____

3. Which declension has mostly feminine nouns? _____

4. What does *mūrus* mean? _____

5. What does *praeda* mean? _____

6. Which one (*mūrus* or *praeda*) would a pirate rather have? _____

C. Conjugate the following verbs in the present tense.

_____ Conjugation or "_____" Family

	SINGULAR	PLURAL
1ST	putō	
2ND		
3RD		

_____ Conjugation or "_____" Family

	SINGULAR	PLURAL
1ST	parō	
2ND		
3RD		

D. Translate the following sentences. In each sentence, underline the verb ending.

1. Recuperāmus. _____

2. Princeps superābit. _____

3. Mūrī stābunt. _____

4. Captīvī parābant. _____

5. Equus exercēbat. _____

6. Iuvābam. _____

7. Urbs manet. _____

8. Hispānia oppugnābit. _____

E. Give the Latin word that each of these English words is derived from. Use this week's Word List.

1. mural _____

4. recuperate _____

2. vulnerable _____

5. campus _____

3. prince _____

F. Answer the questions about this week's quotation.

1. What does *Hannibal ad portās* mean? _____

_____

2. What people used to say this? _____

3. Why did they say it? _____

G. Find and circle the hidden vocabulary words!

vicus	paro	murus	moenia	praefectus
captivus	praeda	princeps	campus	recupero
puto	castra	vulnus	supero	exerceo

```
v  a  r  p  r  a  e  f  e  c  t  u  s  w
u  d  q  e  t  j  s  u  p  e  r  o  m  q
l  i  v  i  c  u  s  c  d  e  e  s  o  m
n  o  e  h  a  r  g  o  i  a  c  g  p  o
u  y  v  a  s  h  i  m  u  r  u  s  r  e
s  d  p  u  t  o  e  h  z  i  p  e  a  n
e  g  h  d  r  o  o  e  w  a  e  s  e  i
q  b  c  p  a  r  o  u  k  o  r  v  d  a
u  a  v  b  g  e  p  j  y  u  o  b  a  j
c  a  p  t  i  v  u  s  a  s  l  n  t  i
k  l  y  o  p  w  p  r  i  n  c  e  p  s
e  x  e  r  c  e  o  m  d  t  r  m  w  u
i  a  c  a  m  p  u  s  h  d  e  l  c  a
```

WEEK 17

Word List:

NOUNS

1. exercitus . . . . army
2. fāma, -ae. . . . . report, reputation
3. hostis . . . . enemy
4. iniūria, -ae . . . . injury
5. lēgātus, -ī . . . . lieutenant
6. nuntius, -ī . . . . message, messenger
7. pugna, -ae . . . . fight
8. sagitta, -ae . . . . arrow
9. sīca, -ae. . . . . dagger
10. triumphus, -ī. . . . . . triumph

ADJECTIVES

11. antīquus . . . . ancient
12. ferus. . . . . fierce, wild

VERBS

13. iubeō (iubēre) . . . . I order
14. noceō (nocēre) . . . . . . I harm
15. perturbō (perturbāre) . . . . I confuse

Chant:

Future Passive Verb Endings

| | LATIN | | | ENGLISH | |
	SINGULAR	PLURAL		SINGULAR	PLURAL
1ST	-bor	-bimur		I will be *verbed*	we will be *verbed*
2ND	-beris	-biminī		you will be *verbed*	you all will be *verbed*
3RD	-bitur	-buntur		he/she/it will be *verbed*	they will be *verbed*

Quotation:

terra incognita—"unknown land"

Weekly Worksheet 17

name: _____

A. Answer the following questions about nouns.

1. What is the definition of a noun? A noun _____

_____ .

2. Translate these words and circle the nouns.

a) nuntius _____   b) exercitus _____

c) perturbō _____   d) lēgātus _____

3. This is more difficult. In one of these sentences, "fight" is a noun, and in the other it is a verb. Underline the sentence where "fight" is used like *pugna*.

a) The fight was fierce.   b) The armies will fight tomorrow.

4. Is *pugna* a noun or a verb? _____

5. Which declension is it in? _____

B. Use a dictionary and write the definition of these English words on the lines below. In the parentheses, write the Latin words from which each word is derived.

1. hostile: _____

_____ (_____)

2. antique: _____

_____ (_____)

3. famous: _____

_____ (_____)

C. Underline the verb, then translate the following sentences into English.

1. Nuntiī perturbant. _____

2. Lēgātus ambulat. _____

3. Sagittae volant. _____

4. Sedet canis. _____

5. Oppugnat exercitus. _____

D. Underline the noun that goes with the verb and then translate the sentences.

NOUN	VERB	TRANSLATION
1. Captīvus / Captīvī	putant.	_____
2. Praefectus / Praefectī	recuperābat.	_____
3. Lēgātus / Lēgātī	superat.	_____
4. Sagitta / Sagittae	perturbābunt.	_____
5. Sīca / Sīcae	nocēbit.	_____

E. Complete this week's chant and answer the questions about it.

	SINGULAR	PLURAL
1ST	-bor	
2ND		
3RD		

1. Are these endings for a verb or a noun? _____

2. What is the name of this chant? _____

F. Answer the questions about this week's quotation.

1. What is the English translation of *terra incognita*? _____

2. Where would you usually find this phrase? _____

WEEK 18

Word List:

NOUNS

1. colōnus, -ī . . . . settler
2. corōna, -ae . . . . crown
3. dux . . . . leader
4. gens . . . . tribe
5. populus, -ī. . . . . people, nation
6. rēgīna, -ae . . . . queen
7. socius, -ī . . . . partner, associate

ADJECTIVES

8. miser . . . . unhappy, wretched,
   miserable
9. potens . . . . powerful

VERBS

10. lēgō (lēgāre) . . . . I appoint
11. negō (negāre) . . . . I deny
12. probō (probāre). . . . . . . I approve
13. prohibeō (prohibēre) . . . . I prevent
14. recūsō (recūsāre) . . . . . . I refuse

ADVERBS

15. nōn . . . . not

Chant:

Imperfect Passive Verb Endings

	LATIN			ENGLISH	
	SINGULAR	PLURAL		SINGULAR	PLURAL
1ST	-bar	-bāmur		I was being *verbed*	we were being *verbed*
2ND	-bāris	-bāminī		you were being *verbed*	you all were being
3RD	-bātur	-bantur		he/she/it was being	they were being *verbed*

(Continued on the next page)

Quotation:

Veni, vidi, vici—"I came, I saw, I conquered"

Weekly Worksheet 18

name:

A. Draw lines to match the Latin words on the left with their English derivatives on the right.

1. gens		prohibit
2. potens		colony
3. corōna		potent
4. dux		Gentile
5. miser		coronation
6. prohibeō		duke
7. colōnus		miser

B. First underline the verb endings, then translate these sentences.

1. Rēgīna probat. _____

2. Rēgīna nōn probat. _____

3. Dux recūsat. _____

4. Dux nōn recūsat. _____

5. Sociī negant. _____

6. Sīca nōn nocēbit. _____

7. Servī flēbant. _____

8. Colōnus nōn respondet. _____

9. Gens lēgat. _____

10. Exercitus exercēbit. _____

C. Answer the questions about this week's quotation.

    1. What is the quotation from this week? _____

    2. What does it mean?_____

D. Which declension is each word in? Use your knowledge of declensions and genitive endings to decide. Then fill in the blank with either 1 (for first delension) or 2 (for second delension).

    1. populus, -ī _____

    2. rēgīna, -ae _____

    3. corōna, -ae _____

    4. socius, -ī _____

    5. sagitta, -ae _____

    6. puer, -ī _____

    7. colōnus, -ī _____

    8. nuntius, -ī _____

    9. puella, -ae _____

    10. captīvus, -ī _____

    11. mūrus, -ī _____

    12. silva, -ae _____

E. Complete this week's chant and answer the questions about it.

	SINGULAR	PLURAL
1ST	-bar	
2ND		
3RD		

    1. What is the name of this chant? _____

    2. Are these verb endings or a complete verb? _____

WEEK 19

Word List:

NOUNS

1. aquila, -ae . . . . eagle
2. aura, -ae . . . . breeze
3. herba, -ae . . . . . . herb, plant
4. lupus, -ī . . . . wolf
5. nimbus, -ī . . . . . . cloud
6. rīpa, -ae . . . . bank (of a creek or river)
7. spēlunca, -ae . . . . . cave
8. taurus, -ī . . . . bull

VERBS

9. dēlectō (dēlectāre). . . . I delight
10. explōrō (explōrāre). . . I find out, explore
11. flōreō (flōrēre) . . . . . . I flourish
12. occultō (occultāre) . . . I hide

ADVERBS

13. bene. . . . . well
14. clam . . . . secretly
15. satis . . . . enough

Chant:

No new chant this week.

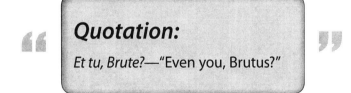

> ## Quotation:
> *Et tu, Brute?*—"Even you, Brutus?"

Weekly Worksheet 19

name:

A. Use what you know about these derivatives to complete the sentences.

1. A *spelunker* is someone who explores _____.

2. A person with an *aquiline* nose has a nose like an _____.

3. If you are *satisfied*, you've had _____.

4. Someone who is using *herbicide* is trying to kill certain _____.

5. A *benefactor* is someone who helps you and wishes you _____.

B. Translate the following words from English to Latin using this week's Word List.

1. breeze _____

5. bull _____

2. eagle _____

6. banks _____

3. clouds _____

7. plant _____

4. caves _____

8. wolf _____

C. Translate the following sentences.

1. Taurus oppugnābat. _____

2. Aquilae bene volant. _____

3. Clam occultātis. _____

4. Lūna dēlectat. _____

5. Lupus clam spectat. _____

6. Exercitī nōn occultābunt. _____

7. Herbae nōn flōrēbant. _____

8. Satis explōrāmus. _____

D. First underline the pronouns, then translate the verbs from English to Latin. (Hint: Notice which ending they all have!)

1. it flourishes _____   4. she finds out _____

2. he hides _____   5. he delights _____

3. he approves_____   6. she refuses _____

E. Answer the questions about this week's quotation.

1. Who said, *Et tu, Brute?* _____

2. What does it mean?_____

F. Give the genitive singular ending of each noun.

1. lupus _____   4. rīpa _____

2. aura _____   5. spēlunca _____

3. taurus _____   6. socius _____

G. Using an encylopedia or the internet, draw a map of Italy in the space below. Label the city of Rome and also the Alps.

WEEK 20

Word List:

NOUNS

1. auxilium, -ī . . . . help, aid
2. beneficium, -ī . . . . . . kindness
3. dōnum, -ī . . . . gift
4. folium, -ī . . . . leaf
5. pābulum, -ī . . . . fodder, food for animals
6. pīlum, -ī . . . . javelin
7. praemium, -ī . . . . . . reward
8. regnum, -ī . . . . kingdom
9. saxum, -ī . . . . rock
10. scūtum, -ī . . . . shield
11. signum, -ī . . . . sign
12. silentium, -ī . . . . silence
13. stagnum, -ī . . . . pond
14. tēlum, -ī . . . . weapon
15. verbum, -ī . . . . word

Chant:

Second Declension Neuter Noun Endings

	LATIN			ENGLISH	
	SINGULAR	PLURAL		SINGULAR	PLURAL
NOM.	-um	-a		a, the *noun*	the *nouns*
GEN.	-ī	-ōrum		of the *noun*, the *noun's*	of the *nouns*, the *nouns'*
DAT.	-ō	-īs		to, for the *noun*	to, for the *nouns*
ACC.	-um	-a		the *noun*	the *nouns*
ABL.	-ō	-īs		by, with, from the *noun*	by, with, from the *nouns*

Quotation:

Excelsior—"ever upward"
(Motto for the state of New York)

Weekly Worksheet 20 name:

A. Fill in the rest of this week's chant, then answer the questions about it.

	SINGULAR	PLURAL
NOM.	-um	
GEN.		
DAT.		
ACC.		
ABL.		

Circle the answer.

1. What is the *genitive singular* ending of all second declension nouns?

    a) -us   b) -ae   c) -ī

2. What is the *nominative singular* ending of all second declension neuter nouns?

    a) -um   b) -us   c) -ī

3. Which declension is *auxilium, -ī* in?

    a) second declension neuter   b) first declension   c) second conjugation

B. Translate the following nouns into Latin. (Hint: They are all second declension neuter nouns!) Notice that some of the words are plural.

1. words _____

2. gift _____

3. kindness _____

4. kingdom _____

5. rocks _____

6. shield _____

7. rewards _____

8. leaf _____

C. Underline the noun that goes with the verb and then translate the sentences.

NOUN	VERB	TRANSLATION
1. Dōnum / Dōna	delectant.	_____
2. Signum / Signa	perturbābant.	_____
3. Regnum / Regna	augēbit.	_____
4. Tēlum / Tēla	nocet.	_____

D. Choose three of these derivatives to look up in an English dictionary. Write down each derivative and its definition on the lines. In the parentheses, write the derivative's Latin root.

foliage   beneficial   premium   stagnant   pabulum   regnant   verb

1. _____ : _____

_____ (_____)

2. _____ : _____

_____ (_____)

3. _____ : _____

_____ (_____)

E. Translate the following second declension neuter nouns.

1. caelum _____   5. bracchium _____

2. oppidum _____   6. aedificium _____

3. perīculum _____   7. bellum _____

4. castellum _____   8. solum _____

F. Answer the questions about this week's quotation.

1. What does *Excelsior* mean? _____

2. What state uses this word as its motto? _____

G. Give the genitive singular ending of each noun, then write whether it is first declension (1), second declension (2), or second declension neuter (2N).

1. stagnum _____-ī___2N_____   6. verbum _____

2. lupus _____   7. pābulum _____

3. pīlum _____   8. herba _____

4. aquila _____   9. taurus _____

5. dōnum _____   10. spēlunca _____

H. Decline *dōnum, -ī.*

	SINGULAR	PLURAL
NOM.	dōnum	
GEN.		
DAT.		
ACC.		
ABL.		

WEEK 21

Word List:

NOUNS

1. aquārius, -ī . . . . water-carrier
2. ariēs . . . . ram
3. aurīga, -ae . . . . charioteer
4. aurōra, -ae . . . . dawn
5. cancer, -crī . . . . crab
6. geminus, -ī . . . . twin
7. leō . . . . lion
8. lībra, -ae . . . . pair of scales
9. piscis . . . . fish
10. sagittārius, -ī . . . . . . archer

11. scorpius, -ī . . . . scorpion
12. ursa, -ae *or* ursus, -ī . . . bear
13. virgō . . . . maiden

ADJECTIVES

14. austrālis . . . . southern
15. borēus, -a, -um . . . . . northern
16. māior . . . . greater
17. minor . . . . smaller

Chant:

No new chant this week.

Quotation:

No quotation this week.

Weekly Worksheet 21

name:

(Test Practice / Weeks 15-21)

A. In boxes below, write the endings for the following declensions:

First Declension

	SINGULAR	PLURAL
NOM.	-a	
GEN.		
DAT.		
ACC.		
ABL.		

Second Declension

SINGULAR	PLURAL
-us	

Second Declension Neuter

SINGULAR	PLURAL
-um	

B. Give the singular and plural forms of these nouns in Latin.

	SINGULAR	PLURAL
1. water carrier	_____	_____
2. archer	_____	_____
3. scorpion	_____	_____
4. messenger	_____	_____
5. son	_____	_____
6. javelin	_____	_____
7. pond	_____	_____
8. charioteer	_____	_____

D. Answer the following questions about derivatives from this week's Word List.

1. What country got its name from the Latin word for "southern"? _____

2. Look at your Word List. What is another name for the Northern Lights, based on two words from the list? _____

E. Draw a line to match each picture with the correct Latin word.

1.   leō

2.   ariēs

3.   piscis

4.   cancer

F. Translate the following sentences into English.

1. Scorpius nocet. _____

2. Piscis volat. _____

3. Sagittāriī bene occultābant. _____

4. Ursae clam florent. _____

5. Aquārius saepe labōrant. _____

G. Translate the following sentences into Latin.

1. The lion frightens. _____

2. The maiden praises. _____

3. The twins laugh. _____

H. Find and circle the hidden vocabulary words!

geminus	ursa	scorpius	lībra	aquarius
sagittarius	auriga	aurora	piscis	virgo
aries	cancer	maior	minor	

```
r  b  x  i  m  p  e  v  f  e  a  m  k  o  h
o  u  s  a  g  i  t  t  a  r  i  u  s  y  u
u  p  o  i  f  s  e  p  b  c  m  a  i  o  r
z  m  e  d  u  c  n  b  a  x  r  u  v  c  q
c  i  a  r  l  i  q  s  l  w  c  n  d  h  u
w  n  f  u  r  s  a  j  a  u  r  i  g  a  w
g  o  a  b  m  a  u  n  m  l  e  v  c  b  i
i  r  m  s  c  o  r  p  i  u  s  w  n  f  l
g  v  o  k  n  g  o  h  i  l  a  p  h  o  t
l  i  b  r  a  t  r  p  g  e  m  i  n  u  s
j  r  k  i  v  c  a  n  c  e  r  u  j  k  r
e  g  y  b  f  i  y  x  h  q  c  l  f  z  d
f  o  u  z  a  q  u  a  r  i  u  s  n  o  u
a  d  r  e  t  t  w  k  o  m  a  r  i  e  s
```

Crossword

Complete the crossword puzzle! Write in the Latin word for each clue.

ACROSS

1. you all increase
15. you delight
22. we refuse
28. well
33. I stand
40. I confuse
43. he hides
44. he trains
45. I write
46. you all help
47. they attack
48. she shares
49. I order
50. I do
51. it flourishes
52. he sets free
53. I give
54. they approve
55. you hope
56. I think
57. I conquer
58. you prepare
59. they give
60. they prevent
61. he deserves
62. I appoint
63. we harm
64. you find out
65. I see
66. they fear
67. you all remain
68. you deny

DOWN

1. building
2. kingdoms
3. road
4. leader
5. breeze
6. herbs
7. mountain
8. crowns
9. pair of scales
10. bulls
11. weapons
12. partner
13. eagle
14. charioteers
15. lord, master
16. lion
17. water-carrier
18. captive
19. soldier
20. scorpion
21. twins
22. queens
23. female bear
24. wall
25. northern
26. caves
27. towns
28. kindness
29. leaves
30. message
31. city

32. dawn
33. shield
34. arrows
35. silence
36. word
37. gifts
38. enemy
39. help, aid
40. rewards
41. camp
42. citizen

What is the only word in the "Across" list that is not a verb?

_____

What is the only word in the "Down" list that is not a noun?

_____

4 UNIT FOUR

UNIT 4: GOALS

By the end of Week 27, you should be able to . . .

- Chant from memory the demonstrative and personal pronoun chants
- Give the meanings for newly learned Latin words
- Translate sentences involving adjectives (e.g., *Populi improbi nōn florent* means "Wicked nations do not flourish")

WEEK 22

Word List:

NOUNS

1. adulēscēns. . . . . young man

2. animus, -ī . . . . mind

3. avus, -ī . . . . grandfather

4. disciplīna, -ae . . . . . . instruction, training

5. patientia, -ae . . . . . . patience

ADJECTIVES

6. beātus, -a, -um . . . . . . happy, blessed

7. contentus, -a, -um . . . . satisfied, content

8. honestus, -a, -um . . . . honorable

9. improbus, -a, -um . . . . wicked

10. stultus, -a, -um . . . . . foolish

VERBS

11. appellō (appellāre) . . . I name

12. errō (errāre) . . . . I wander

13. placeō (placēre). . . . . I please

14. recitō (recitāre) . . . . . I read aloud

15. rogō (rogāre) . . . . . . I ask

Chant:

Hic, haec, hoc: *this*
Singular Demonstrative Pronouns / Adjectives

| LATIN | | | | ENGLISH |
	MASCULINE	FEMININE	NEUTER		SINGULAR
NOM.	hic	haec	hoc		this
GEN.	huius	huius	huius		of this
DAT.	huic	huic	huic		to, for this
ACC.	hunc	hanc	hoc		this
ABL.	hōc	hāc	hōc		by, with, from this

(Continued on the next page)

Quotation:

Cogito ergo sum—"I think, therefore I am"

Weekly Worksheet 22   *name:*

A. Conjugate the following verbs and answer the questions about them.

	SINGULAR	PLURAL
1ST	amō	
2ND		
3RD		

1. *Amō* is in the _____ conjugation or "_____" family.

2. *Amō* means _____.

3. Is *amō* in the present, imperfect, or future tense? _____

	SINGULAR	PLURAL
1ST	placēbō	
2ND		
3RD		

4. Is *placēbō* the present, imperfect, or future tense form of *placēbō*? _____

5. *Placēbō* is in the _____ conjugation or "_____" family.

6. *Placēbō* means _____ .

	SINGULAR	PLURAL
1ST	rogābam	
2ND		
3RD		

7. Is *rogābam* the present, imperfect, or future tense form of *rogō*? _____

8. *Rogō* is in the _____ conjugation or "_____" family.

9. *Rogābam* means _____ .

B. For 1–4, underline each verb's ending and translate it. For 5–6, translate the English into Latin.

1. ambulātis _____   4. placet _____

2. appellant _____   5. we were naming _____

3. recitābō _____   6. you wander _____

C. Below is a list of singular adjectives. Adjectives can have masculine, feminine, or neuter endings. Decide which ending each adjective has, and then write in the blank M (masculine), F (feminine), or N (neuter).

1. beātus _____   4. honesta _____

2. stultum _____   5. improbum _____

3. contenta _____   6. longus _____

D. Below are noun and adjective phrases in Latin. For each phrase, underline the noun's ending, and circle the ending on the adjective. Then translate each phrase. (Hint: The last two phrases are plural.)

1. honestus avus _____

2. stultus animus _____

3. beāta patientia _____

4. improba rēgīna _____

5. honestum regnum _____

6. beāta signa _____

7. improbī geminī _____

E. Each sentence below uses an adjective and a form of *sum*. Translate each sentence. This will be easiest if you begin by translating the verb. (Hint: The subject gender and adjective gender must match!) The first one is done for you.

1. Stultus est. _____ He is foolish. _____

2. Contentus sum. _____

3. Beāta sum. _____

4. Beātus es. _____

5. Honestus est. _____

6. Improbus est. _____

F. Translate this week's quotation.

1. *Cōgitō ergo sum.* _____

2. Who was the French philosopher who said this? _____

G. Fill in the missing words in this week's chant, then answer the questions.

	MASCULINE	FEMININE	NEUTER
NOM.	hic	haec	
GEN.	huius		huius
DAT.	huic	huic	
ACC.		hanc	
ABL.	hōc		

1. What does *hic* mean? _____

2. Is *hic* singular or plural? _____

WEEK 23

Word List:

NOUNS

1. ancora, -ae. . . . . anchor
2. classis. . . . . fleet (of ships)
3. iter . . . . journey
4. ōra, -ae . . . . shore
5. pons . . . . bridge
6. portus . . . . harbor
7. rēmus, -ī . . . . oar
8. tempestās . . . . weather, storm
9. unda, -ae. . . . . wave
10. vēlum, -ī . . . . sail
11. ventus, -ī . . . . wind

ADJECTIVES

12. aequus, -a, -um . . . . . level, even, calm
13. lātus, -a, -um. . . . . . . wide, broad

VERBS

14. nō (nāre) . . . . I swim

ADVERBS

15. prope . . . . near

Chant:

Hī, hae, haec: *these*
Plural Demonstrative Pronouns / Adjectives

	LATIN				ENGLISH
	MASCULINE	FEMININE	NEUTER		PLURAL
NOM.	hī	hae	haec		these
GEN.	hōrum	hārum	hōrum		of these
DAT.	hīs	hīs	hīs		to, for these
ACC.	hōs	hās	haec		these
ABL.	hīs	hīs	hīs		by, with, from these

(Continued on the next page)

Quotation:

Deō volente—"God willing"

Weekly Worksheet 23   *name:*

A. Write the rest of this chant in the box, then answer the questions. Can you do it from memory?

	MASCULINE	FEMININE	NEUTER
NOM.	hī	hae	haec
GEN.			
DAT.			
ACC.			
ABL.			

1. Is *hī* singular or plural? _____

2. What does it mean? _____

B. Underline the adjective that goes with the noun and then translate the phrase.

ADJECTIVE	NOUN	TRANSLATION
1. Lātus / Lāta	unda	_____
2. Lātum / Lāta	vēlum	_____
3. Aequa / Aequum	libra	_____
4. Magnī / Magnae	ancorae	_____
5. Fera / Ferī	ventī	_____

C. Translate these sentences. Watch for adverbs and adjectives!

1. Ventus auget. _____

2. Tempestās saepe mūtat. _____

3. Classis errat. _____

4. Piscis nat. _____

5. Nautae clāmant et labōrant. _____

6. Undae magnae sunt. _____

7. Ancora nōn movēbit. _____

8. Mare aequum nōn est. _____

9. Lātī vēlī volant. _____

10. Aequa est. _____

11. Portus prope est. _____

12. Rēmī antīquī sunt. _____

D. Circle the correct meaning of these derivatives.

1. An *itinerary* is:

a) a menu.   b) a lengthy letter.   c) the route of a journey.

2. If a field of grass is *undulating*, it is:

a) parched from drought.   b) flourishing.   c) waving in the wind.

3. A *tempest* is a:

a) violent rainstorm.   b) lacy curtain.   c) high riverbank.

4. When you *ventilate* a room, you are letting in:

a) bugs.   b) air.   c) rain.

E. Fill in the blank.

1. *Deō Volente* is sometimes abbreviated "D.V." It means _____ .

F. Below, draw all of these things in a picture and label them: *ancora, nauta, remus, ora, unda, tempestas, nāvis, classis, portus, saxum.*

WEEK 24

Word List:

NOUNS

1. apostolus, -ī . . . . apostle
2. Biblia Sacra . . . . Holy Bible
3. Christus, -ī . . . . Christ
4. ecclēsia, -ae . . . . church
5. ēvangelium, -ī . . . . . . good news
6. fidēs . . . . faith
7. Iesus. . . . . Jesus
8. mors . . . . death
9. pax . . . . peace
10. poena, -ae . . . . penalty, punishment
11. spēs . . . . hope

ADJECTIVES

12. vērus, -a, -um . . . . . . true
13. vīvus, -a, -um . . . . . . living

VERBS

14. crēdō . . . . I believe
15. praedīcō . . . . I proclaim

Chants:

Ego, nōs: *I, we*
Personal Pronouns

LATIN

	SINGULAR	PLURAL
NOM.	ego	nōs
GEN.	meī	nostrum
DAT.	mihi	nōbīs
ACC.	mē	nōs
ABL.	mē	nōbīs

ENGLISH

	SINGULAR	PLURAL
NOM.	I	we
GEN.	of me	of us
DAT.	to, for me	to, for us
ACC.	me	us
ABL.	by, with, from me	by, with, from us

(Continued on the next page)

Tū, vōs: *you, you all*

Personal Pronouns

	SINGULAR	PLURAL		SINGULAR	PLURAL
NOM.	tū	vōs		you	you all
GEN.	tuī	vestrum		of you	of you all
DAT.	tibi	vōbīs		to, for you	to, for you all
ACC.	tē	vōs		you	you all
ABL.	tē	vōbīs		by, with, from you	by, with, from you all

Quotation:

Iesus Nazarenus, Rex Iudaeorum—"Jesus the Nazarene, King of the Jews"

Weekly Worksheet 24 *name:*

A. Complete this week's chants, then answer the questions. Try to do it from memory!

	SINGULAR	PLURAL
NOM.	ego	nōs
GEN.		
DAT.		
ACC.		
ABL.		

	SINGULAR	PLURAL
NOM.	tū	vōs
GEN.		
DAT.		
ACC.		
ABL.		

1. Are *ego, nōs, tū* and *vōs* nouns, pronouns, or adjectives? _____

2. Is *ego* first, second, or third person? _____

3. What does *ego* mean? _____

4. What does *nōs* mean? _____

5. Is *tū* first, second, or third person? _____

6. What does *tū* mean? _____

7. What does *vōs* mean? _____

B. Complete the charts below.

First Declension

	SINGULAR	PLURAL
NOM.	-a	
GEN.		
DAT.		
ACC.		
ABL.		

Second Declension

	SINGULAR	PLURAL
	-us	

C. Give the singular and plural forms of these nouns in Latin.

	SINGULAR	PLURAL
1. penalty	_____	_____
2. church	_____	_____
3. apostle	_____	_____
4. anchor	_____	_____
5. shore	_____	_____

D. Translate these words from this week's Word List into English, and indicate whether each is a noun, verb, or adjective (parts of speech).

	TRANSLATION	PART OF SPEECH
1. vērus, -a, -um	_____	_____
2. crēdō	_____	_____
3. praedīcō	_____	_____
4. fidēs	_____	_____
5. vīvus, -a, -um	_____	_____

E. Label the columns singular or plural and indicate first, second, and third person. Then conjugate *probō* in the present tense.

F. Translate the following sentences.

1. Iesus vīvus est. _____

2. Ēvangelium vērum est. _____

3. Apostolus beātus recitat. _____

4. Lupus improbus errābat. _____

5. Insulae parvae sunt. _____

6. Nōn praedīcō. _____

7. Magnae herbae flōrēbant. _____

8. Equus parvus potest. _____

G. Answer the following questions about this week's quotation.

1. Translate *Iesus Nazarenus, Rex Iudaeorum.* _____

_____

2. Where was this originally posted? _____

WEEK 25

Word List:

NOUNS

1. agricola, -ae . . . . . . farmer
2. animal . . . . animal
3. cibus, -ī . . . . food
4. famēs . . . . hunger, famine, starvation
5. fossa, -ae . . . . ditch
6. hortus, -ī . . . . garden
7. pastor . . . . shepherd
8. pulvis . . . . dirt, dust, powder
9. sēmen . . . . seed

10. stabulum, -ī . . . . . . stall, stable
11. villa, -ae . . . . farmhouse, country house
12. vīnum, -ī . . . . wine

ADJECTIVES

13. albus, -a, -um . . . . . white

VERBS

14. serō . . . . I sow, plant
15. vulnerō (vulnerāre) . . . I wound

Chant:

No new chant this week.

Quotation:

Sic semper tyrannis—"Thus always to tyrants"
(Motto for the state of Virginia)

Weekly Worksheet 25

name:

A. Sort the following words into the four lists: people, places people live, animals, and places animals live.

ager, agricola, rēgīna, lupus, urbs, cīvis, ursa, equus, castellum, mare, domus, māter, spēlunca, stabulum, piscis, silva, villa, avis, nauta, nāvis

People

Places People Live

Animals

Places Animals Live

B. There are three words from this week's list which have English derivatives that are spelled exactly the same in both languages. List them below.

1. _____   2. _____   3. _____

C. Conjugate *vulnerō (vulnerāre)* in the present tense and give its translation.

	LATIN			ENGLISH	
	SINGULAR	**PLURAL**		**SINGULAR**	**PLURAL**
1ST					
2ND					
3RD					

D. Answer the following questions about this week's quotation.

1. What does *sic semper tyrannis* mean? _____

2. Which state uses this quotation as its motto? _____

E. Translate these sentences into English. The last sentences uses two adjectives!

1. Beātī sumus. _____

2. Puella parva nat. _____

3. Adulēscēns clam rogābit. _____

4. Scorpiī ferī oppugnant. _____

5. Equus magnus albus errat. _____

F. Give the plural forms of these phrases in Latin, then translate what you have written.

	PLURAL	TRANSLATION
1. puer et puella	_____	_____
2. albus nimbus	_____	_____
3. lātum vēlum	_____	_____
4. parva villa	_____	_____

WEEK 26

Word List:

NOUNS

1. forum, -ī . . . . public square, marketplace
2. īra, -ae . . . . anger
3. lingua, -ae . . . . language
4. rēs . . . . thing
5. sacculus, -ī . . . . little bag
6. sententia, -ae . . . . . . opinion
7. toga, -ae . . . . toga
8. vox . . . . voice

ADJECTIVES

9. aliēnus, -a, -um . . . . . . foreign
10. mediocris . . . . ordinary
11. mīrus, -a, -um . . . . . . strange, wonderful

VERBS

12. censeō (censēre) . . . . I estimate
13. postulō (postulāre) . . . I demand
14. vītō (vītāre) . . . . I avoid

PREPOSITIONS

15. inter . . . . between

Chant:

No new chant this week.

Quotation:

In hōc signō vinces—"In this sign you will conquer"

Weekly Worksheet 26   *name:*

A. Conjugate *censeō* in the present tense, then answer the questions about it.

	SINGULAR	PLURAL
1ST		
2ND		
3RD		

1. *Censeō* is in the _____ conjugation or the "_____" family.

2. What tense is *censeō*—present, imperfect, or future? _____

3. How would you say, "You are estimating"? _____

4. Which form of *censeō* would you use in the sentence, "The sailors estimate"? _____

B. Underline the ending of each verb, then translate it.

1. vītāmus _____   4. vītābant _____

2. postulābīmus _____   5. postulat _____

3. censēbunt _____   6. censētis _____

C. Translate these sentences.

1. Agricolae censent. _____

2. Adulēscēns vītat. _____

3. Cīvis saepe postulābit. _____

4. Fossa magna est. _____

5. Aliēna lingua perturbat. _____

6. Togae antīquae sunt. _____

7. Forum magnum et lātum est. _____

8. Hortus mīrus flōrēbat. _____

D. Circle the meaning of the derivatives from this week's Word List.

1. If something is *mediocre*, it is:

   a) very interesting.   b) just the usual.   c) bright.

2. *Linguistics* is:

   a) the study of rain.   b) an Italian food.   c) the science of language.

3. If a danger is *inevitable*, it can't:

   a) be seen.   b) be avoided.   c) be overcome.

4. When somone is *irate,* it means they are:

   a) poor.   b) wonderful.   c) angry.

E. Answer the questions about this week's quotation.

1. Translate: *In hōc signō vinces* _____

2. According to legend, who first saw these words in a vision? _____

F. Fill in the blanks with the present passive verb endings.

	SINGULAR	PLURAL
1ST		
2ND		
3RD		

WEEK 27

Word List:

NOUNS

1. annus, -ī . . . . year
2. fīnis . . . . the end
3. hōra, -ae . . . . hour
4. mensis . . . . month
5. merīdiēs . . . . noon
6. tempus. . . . . time

ADJECTIVES

7. multus, -a, -um . . . . . . much, many
8. prīmus, -a, -um . . . . . . first

VERBS

9. sciō . . . . I know

ADVERBS

10. ante . . . . before
11. crās . . . . tomorrow
12. herī . . . . yesterday
13. hodiē . . . . today
14. post . . . . after

INTERJECTIONS

15. ecce . . . . behold!

Chant:

No new chant this week.

Quotation:

A.M., *ante merīdiem*— "before noon"

P.M., *post merīdiem*—"after noon"

Weekly Worksheet 27

name:

A. Fill in these blanks to answer the questions about derivatives from this week's list.

1. *Annual* comes from the Latin word _____.

2. If something happens *annually*, it happens every _____.

3. *Multitude* is a derivative of _____.

4. When Jesus talked to the *multitudes*, he was talking to _____ people.

5. *Procrastinate* is derived from _____.

6. When you *procrastinate,* you put something off until _____.

7. The word *premier* comes from the Latin _____.

8. At a movie's *premier*, it is being shown for the _____ time.

B. For each sentence, label the Subject Noun (SN) and Verb (V) and underline the verb's ending. Then translate the sentence.

1. Avus saepe recitat. _____

2. Adulēscēns nōn rogābit. _____

3. Ecclēsiae semper ōrant. _____

4. Ursae multae manēbunt. _____

5. Tempus volat. (You could also say *tempus fugit*.) _____

6. Fossa longa est. _____

7. Puellae parvae simulant. _____

Extra credit: Prīmus est. _____

C. These are Latin abbreviations. Give the unabbreviated Latin and then the translation.

LATIN   TRANSLATION

1. A.M. _____   _____

2. P.M. _____   _____

3. A.D. _____   _____

4. P.S. _____   _____

D. Answer the following questions about quotations.

1. What does *ante bellum* mean? _____

2. In the Latin translation of the Bible, when Pilate brings Jesus out before the people, Pilate says

"Ecce homō!" What does this mean? _____

E. Underline the adjective that goes with the noun and then translate the phrase.

ADJECTIVE   NOUN   TRANSLATION

1. Prīmus / Prīmī   annus   _____

2. Multī / Multae   hōrae   _____

3. Magnum / Magnus   folium   _____

4. Mīra / Mīrae   sententiae   _____

5. Album / Albus   vīnum   _____

F. Find and circle the hidden vocabulary words!

annus	tempus	hora	mensis	hodie
meridies	ante	post	heri	cras
multus	primus	scio	ecce	finis

```
a n n u s e f j n o f d z t
r g k m c j n v h e r i c k
h m f b i h m e t b y t f m
j e e c o d r q k d h e u p
t r b f r s f i n i s m k o
x i h o d i e c l n v p d s
c d s d x d s z q u g u x t
r i c m g f m u l t u s z k
a e s v c s d m r n s w h d
s s f o m e n s i s a j e f
z e h p r i m u s c t g c w
p a n t e x f b h j v r c e
s j d w s h o r a m x f e t
```

APPENDICES

- Weekly Journal
- Contemporary Latin References
- Chant Charts
- Glossary
- Sources and Helps

WEEKLY JOURNAL

Derivatives and Quotations

Each week, write down the derivatives and quotation you have learned.

UNIT 1

Week 1 *Derivatives:* _____

_____

_____

Quotation: _____

_____

Week 2 *Derivatives:* _____

_____

_____

Quotation: _____

_____

Week 3 *Derivatives:* _____

_____

_____

Quotation: _____

_____

Week 4 *Derivatives:* _____

_____

Quotation: _____

Week 5 *Derivatives:* _____

Quotation: _____

Week 6 *Derivatives:* _____

Quotation: _____

Week 7 *Derivatives:* _____

Quotation: There is no quotation for this week.

UNIT 2

Week 8 *Derivatives:* _____

Quotation: _____

_____

Week 9 *Derivatives:* _____

_____

_____

Quotation: _____

_____

Week 10 *Derivatives:* _____

_____

_____

Quotation: _____

_____

Week 11 *Derivatives:* _____

_____

_____

Quotation: _____

_____

Week 12 *Derivatives:* _____

_____

_____

Quotation: _____

_____

Week 13 *Derivatives:* _____

_____

_____

Quotation: _____

_____

Week 14 *Derivatives:* _____

_____

_____

Quotation: There is no quotation for this week.

UNIT 3

Week 15 *Derivatives:* _____

_____

_____

Quotation: _____

_____

Week 16 *Derivatives:* _____

_____

_____

Quotation: _____

_____

Week 17 *Derivatives:* _____

_____

Quotation: _____

_____

Week 18 _Derivatives:_ _____

_____

_____

Quotation: _____

_____

Week 19 _Derivatives:_ _____

_____

_____

Quotation: _____

_____

Week 20 _Derivatives:_ _____

_____

_____

Quotation: _____

_____

Week 21 _Derivatives:_ _____

_____

_____

Quotation: There is no quotation for this week.

UNIT 4

Week 22 *Derivatives:* _____

_____

_____

Quotation: _____

_____

Week 23 *Derivatives:* _____

_____

_____

Quotation: _____

_____

Week 24 *Derivatives:* _____

_____

_____

Quotation: _____

_____

Week 25 *Derivatives:* _____

_____

_____

Quotation: _____

_____

Week 26 *Derivatives:* _____

_____

_____

Quotation: _____

_____

Week 27 *Derivatives:* _____

_____

_____

Quotation: There is no quotation for this week.

CONTEMPORARY LATIN REFERENCES

Number Chart

	LATIN	ITALIAN	SPANISH	FRENCH
1	ūnus	un(o)	un(o)	un
2	duo	due	dos	deux
3	trēs	tre	tres	trois
4	quattuor	quattro	cuatro	quatre
5	quīnque	cinque	cinco	cinq
6	sex	sei	seis	six
7	septem	sette	siete	sept
8	octō	otto	ocho	huit
9	novem	nove	nueve	neuf
10	decem	dieci	diez	dix
11	ūndecim	undici	once	onze
12	duodecim	dodici	doce	douze
100	centum	cento	ciento	cent
1000	mīlle	mille	mil	mille

Constellations

Andromeda	Circinus	Lacerta	Piscis Austrinus
Antlia	Columba	Leo	Puppis
Apus	Coma Berenices	Leo Minor	Pyxis
Aquarius	Corona Austrina	Lepus	Reticulum
Aquila	Corona Borealis	Libra	Sagitta
Ara	Corvus	Lupus	Sagittarius
Aries	Crater	Lynx	Scorpius
Auriga	Crux	Lyra	Sculptor
Boötes	Cygnus	Mensa	Scutum
Caelum	Delphinus	Microscopium	Serpens
Camelopardalis	Dorado	Monoceros	Sextans
Cancer	Draco	Musca	Taurus
Canes Venatici	Equuleus	Norma	Telescopium
Canis Major	Eridanus	Octans	Triangulum
Canis Minor	Fornax	Ophiuchus	Triangulum Australe
Capricornus	Gemini	Orion	Tucana
Carina	Grus	Pavo	Ursa Major
Cassiopeia	Hercules	Pegasus	Ursa Minor
Centaurus	Horologium	Perseus	Vela
Cepheus	Hydra	Phoenix	Virgo
Cetus	Hydrus	Pictor	Volans
Chameleon	Indus	Pisces	Vulpecula

Latin State Mottoes

The mottoes appear here without macrons, as they would in a state's flag or crest.

Arizona: *Ditat Deus*—"God enriches"

Arkansas: *Regnat populus*—"The people rule"

Alabama: *Audemus jura nostra defendere*—"We dare to defend our rights"

Colorado: *Nil sine numine*—"Nothing without providence"

Connecticut: *Qui transtulit sustinet*—"He who transplanted still sustains"

District of Columbia: *Justitia omnibus*—"Justice to all"

Idaho: *Esto perpetua*—"May she be forever"

Kansas: *Ad astra per aspera*—"To the stars through difficulties"

Maine: *Dirigo*—"I direct"

Maryland: *Scuto bonae voluntatis tuae coronasti nos*—"With the shield of thy goodwill Thou has covered us"

Massachusetts: *Ense petit placidam sub libertate quietem*—"By the sword we seek peace, but peace only under liberty"

Boston, Massachusetts: *Sicut patribus, sit Deus nobis*—"As with our fathers, may God be with us"

Michigan: *Si quaeris peninsulam amoenam, circumspice*—"If you seek a pleasant peninsula, look about you"

Mississippi: *Virtute et armis*—"By valor and arms"

Missouri: *Salus populi suprema lex esto*—"The welfare of the people shall be the supreme law"

New Mexico: *Crescit eundo*—"It grows as it goes"

New York: *Excelsior*—"Ever upward"

North Carolina: *Esse quam videri*—"To be rather than to seem"

Oklahoma: *Labor omnia vincit*—"Labor conquers all things"

Oregon: *Alis volat propriis*—"She flies on her own wings"

South Carolina*: *Animis opibusque parati*—"Prepared in minds and resources"

South Carolina*: *Dum spiro, spero*—"While I breathe, I hope"

Virginia: *Sic semper tyrannis*—"Thus always to tyrants"

West Virginia: *Montani semper liberi*—"Mountaineers are always freemen"

Wyoming: *Cedant arma togae*—"Let the arms yield to the toga [diplomacy]"

*South Carolina has two state mottoes.

CHANT CHARTS

Chants, in Order of Memorization

The chants in this section are listed in the order you have learned them.

Amō, *I love*— Present Active
First Conjugation or "ā" Family Verb *(Week 1, p. 4)*

	SINGULAR	PLURAL		SINGULAR	PLURAL
1ST	amō	amāmus		I love	we love
2ND	amās	amātis		you love	you all love
3RD	amat	amant		he/she/it loves	they love

Sum, *I am*— Present Active
Irregular Verb *(Week 2, p. 7)*

	SINGULAR	PLURAL		SINGULAR	PLURAL
1ST	sum	sumus		I am	we are
2ND	es	estis		you are	you all are
3RD	est	sunt		he/she/it is	they are

Present Active Verb Endings *(Week 3, p. 13)*

	SINGULAR	PLURAL		SINGULAR	PLURAL
1ST	-ō	-mus		I am *verbing*, I *verb*	we are *verbing*
2ND	-s	-tis		you are *verbing*	you all are *verbing*
3RD	-t	-nt		he/she/it is *verbing*	they are *verbing*

Future Active Verb Endings *(Week 4, p. 17)*

	SINGULAR	PLURAL		SINGULAR	PLURAL
1ST	-bō	-bimus		I will *verb*	we will *verb*
2ND	-bis	-bitis		you will *verb*	you all will *verb*
3RD	-bit	-bunt		he/she/it will *verb*	they will *verb*

Imperfect Active Verb Endings

(Week 6, p. 31)

	SINGULAR	PLURAL		SINGULAR	PLURAL
1ST	-bam	-bāmus		I was *verbing*	we were *verbing*
2ND	-bās	-bātis		you were *verbing*	you all were *verbing*
3RD	-bat	-bant		he/she/it was *verbing*	they were *verbing*

Videō, *I see*— Present Active

Second Conjugation verb or "ē" Family Verb

(Week 8, p. 45)

	SINGULAR	PLURAL		SINGULAR	PLURAL
1ST	videō	vidēmus		I see	we see
2ND	vidēs	vidētis		you see	you all see
3RD	videt	vident		he/she/it sees	they see

Possum, *I am able*— Present Active

Irregular Verb

(Week 9, p. 51)

	SINGULAR	PLURAL		SINGULAR	PLURAL
1ST	possum	possumus		I am able	we are able
2ND	potes	potestis		you are able	you all are able
3RD	potest	possunt		he/she/it is able	they are able

First Declension Noun Endings

(Week 10, p. 57)

	SINGULAR	PLURAL		SINGULAR	PLURAL
NOM.	-a	-ae		a, the *noun*	the *nouns*
GEN.	-ae	-ārum		of the *noun*, the *noun's*	of the *nouns*, the *nouns'*
DAT.	-ae	-īs		to, for the *noun*	to, for the *nouns*
ACC.	-am	-ās		the *noun*	the *nouns*
ABL.	-ā	-īs		by, with, from the *noun*	by, with, from the *nouns*

Second Declension Noun Endings

(Week 11, p. 63)

	SINGULAR	PLURAL		SINGULAR	PLURAL
NOM.	-us	-ī		a, the *noun*	the *nouns*
GEN.	-ī	-ōrum		of the *noun*, the *noun's*	of the *nouns*, the *nouns'*
DAT.	-ō	-īs		to, for the *noun*	to, for the *nouns*
ACC.	-um	-ōs		the *noun*	the *nouns*
ABL.	-ō	-īs		by, with, from the *noun*	by, with, from the *nouns*

Perfect Active Verb Endings

(Week 12, p. 67)

	SINGULAR	PLURAL		SINGULAR	PLURAL
1ST	-ī	-imus		I have *verbed*	we have *verbed*
2ND	-istī	-istis		you have *verbed*	you all have *verbed*
3RD	-it	-ērunt		he/she/it has *verbed*	they have *verbed*

Future Perfect Active Verb Endings

(Week 13, p. 73)

	SINGULAR	PLURAL		SINGULAR	PLURAL
1ST	-erō	-erimus		I will have *verbed*	we will have *verbed*
2ND	-eris	-eritis		you will have *verbed*	you all will have *verbed*
3RD	-erit	-erint		he/she/it will have *verbed*	they will have *verbed*

Pluperfect Active Verb Endings

(Week 15, p. 89)

	SINGULAR	PLURAL		SINGULAR	PLURAL
1ST	-eram	-erāmus		I had *verbed*	we had *verbed*
2ND	-erās	-eratis		you had *verbed*	you all had *verbed*
3RD	-erat	-erant		he/she/it had *verbed*	they had *verbed*

Present Passive Verb Endings

(Week 16, p. 95)

	SINGULAR	PLURAL		SINGULAR	PLURAL
1ST	-r	-mur		I am being *verbed*	we are being *verbed*
2ND	-ris	-minī		you are being *verbed*	you all are being *verbed*
3RD	-tur	-ntur		he/she/it is being *verbed*	they are being *verbed*

Future Passive Verb Endings

(Week 17, p. 101)

	SINGULAR	PLURAL		SINGULAR	PLURAL
1ST	-bor	-bimur		I will be *verbed*	we will be *verbed*
2ND	-beris	-biminī		you will be *verbed*	you all will be *verbed*
3RD	-bitur	-buntur		he/she/it will be *verbed*	they will be *verbed*

Imperfect Passive Verb Endings

(Week 18, p. 105)

	SINGULAR	PLURAL		SINGULAR	PLURAL
1ST	-bar	-bāmur		I was being *verbed*	we were being *verbed*
2ND	-bāris	-bāminī		you were being *verbed*	you all were being
3RD	-bātur	-bantur		he/she/it was being *verbed*	they were being *verbed*

Second Declension Neuter Noun Endings

(Week 20, p. 113)

	SINGULAR	PLURAL		SINGULAR	PLURAL
NOM.	-um	-a		a, the *noun*	the *nouns*
GEN.	-ī	-ōrum		of the *noun*, the *noun's*	of the *nouns*, the *nouns'*
DAT.	-ō	-īs		to, for the *noun*	to, for the *nouns*
ACC.	-um	-a		the *noun*	the *nouns*
ABL.	-ō	-īs		by, with, from the *noun*	by, with, from the *nouns*

Hic, haec, hoc: *this*

Singular Demonstrative Pronouns / Adjectives

(Week 22, p. 129)

	MASCULINE	FEMININE	NEUTER		SINGULAR
NOM.	hic	haec	hoc		this
GEN.	huius	huius	huius		of this
DAT.	huic	huic	huic		to, for this
ACC.	hunc	hanc	hoc		this
ABL.	hōc	hāc	hōc		by, with, from this

Hī, hae, haec: *these*

Plural Demonstrative Pronouns / Adjectives *(Week 23, p. 135)*

	MASCULINE	FEMININE	NEUTER		PLURAL
NOM.	hī	hae	haec		these
GEN.	hōrum	hārum	hōrum		of these
DAT.	hīs	hīs	hīs		to, for these
ACC.	hōs	hās	haec		these
ABL.	hīs	hīs	hīs		by, with, from these

Ego, nōs: *I, we*

Personal Pronouns *(Week 24, p. 141)*

	SINGULAR	PLURAL		SINGULAR	PLURAL
NOM.	ego	nōs		I	we
GEN.	meī	nostrum		of me, my	of us
DAT.	mihi	nōbīs		to, for me	to, for us
ACC.	mē	nōs		me	us
ABL.	mē	nōbīs		by, with, from me	by, with, from us

Tū, vōs: *you, you all*

Personal Pronouns *(Week 24, p. 142)*

	SINGULAR	PLURAL		SINGULAR	PLURAL
NOM.	tū	vōs		you	you all
GEN.	tuī	vestrum		of you	of you all
DAT.	tibi	vōbīs		to, for you	to, for you all
ACC.	tē	vōs		you	you all
ABL.	tē	vōbīs		by, with, from you	by, with, from you all

Chants, in Order of Parts of Speech

The chants in this section are grouped according to Parts of Speech.

VERBS

Present Active Verb Endings
(Week 3, p. 13)

	SINGULAR	PLURAL		SINGULAR	PLURAL
1ST	-ō	-mus		I am *verbing*, I *verb*	we are *verbing*
2ND	-s	-tis		you are *verbing*	you all are *verbing*
3RD	-t	-nt		he/she/it is *verbing*	they are *verbing*

Future Active Verb Endings
(Week 4, p. 17)

	SINGULAR	PLURAL		SINGULAR	PLURAL
1ST	-bō	-bimus		I will *verb*	we will *verb*
2ND	-bis	-bitis		you will *verb*	you all will *verb*
3RD	-bit	-bunt		he/she/it will *verb*	they will *verb*

Imperfect Active Verb Endings
(Week 6, p. 31)

	SINGULAR	PLURAL		SINGULAR	PLURAL
1ST	-bam	-bāmus		I was *verbing*	we were *verbing*
2ND	-bās	-bātis		you were *verbing*	you all were *verbing*
3RD	-bat	-bant		he/she/it was *verbing*	they were *verbing*

Perfect Active Verb Endings
(Week 12, p. 67)

	SINGULAR	PLURAL		SINGULAR	PLURAL
1ST	-ī	-imus		I have *verbed*	we have *verbed*
2ND	-istī	-istis		you have *verbed*	you all have *verbed*
3RD	-it	-ērunt		he/she/it has *verbed*	they have *verbed*

Future Perfect Active Verb Endings

(Week 13, p. 73)

	SINGULAR	PLURAL		SINGULAR	PLURAL
1ST	-erō	-erimus		I will have *verbed*	we will have *verbed*
2ND	-eris	-eritis		you will have *verbed*	you all will have *verbed*
3RD	-erit	-erint		he/she/it will have *verbed*	they will have *verbed*

Pluperfect Active Verb Endings

(Week 15, p. 89)

	SINGULAR	PLURAL		SINGULAR	PLURAL
1ST	-eram	-erāmus		I had *verbed*	we had *verbed*
2ND	-erās	-eratis		you had *verbed*	you all had *verbed*
3RD	-erat	-erant		he/she/it had *verbed*	they had *verbed*

Present Passive Verb Endings

(Week 16, p. 95)

	SINGULAR	PLURAL		SINGULAR	PLURAL
1ST	-r	-mur		I am being *verbed*	we are being *verbed*
2ND	-ris	-minī		you are being *verbed*	you all are being *verbed*
3RD	-tur	-ntur		he/she/it is being *verbed*	they are being *verbed*

Future Passive Verb Endings

(Week 17, p. 101)

	SINGULAR	PLURAL		SINGULAR	PLURAL
1ST	-bor	-bimur		I will be *verbed*	we will be *verbed*
2ND	-beris	-biminī		you will be *verbed*	you all will be *verbed*
3RD	-bitur	-buntur		he/she/it will be *verbed*	they will be *verbed*

Imperfect Passive Verb Endings

(Week 18, p. 105)

	SINGULAR	PLURAL		SINGULAR	PLURAL
1ST	-bar	-bāmur		I was being *verbed*	we were being *verbed*
2ND	-bāris	-bāminī		you were being *verbed*	you all were being
3RD	-bātur	-bantur		he/she/it was being *verbed*	they were being *verbed*

Amō, *I love*— Present Active

First Conjugation or "ā" Family Verb   *(Week 1, p. 4)*

	SINGULAR	PLURAL		SINGULAR	PLURAL
1ST	amō	amāmus		I love	we love
2ND	amās	amātis		you love	you all love
3RD	amat	amant		he/she/it loves	they love

Videō, *I see*— Present Active

Second Conjugation verb or "ē" Family Verb   *(Week 8, p. 45)*

	SINGULAR	PLURAL		SINGULAR	PLURAL
1ST	videō	vidēmus		I see	we see
2ND	vidēs	vidētis		you see	you all see
3RD	videt	vident		he/she/it sees	they see

Sum, *I am*— Present Active

Irregular Verb   *(Week 2, p. 7)*

	SINGULAR	PLURAL		SINGULAR	PLURAL
1ST	sum	sumus		I am	we are
2ND	es	estis		you are	you all are
3RD	est	sunt		he/she/it is	they are

Possum, *I am able*— Present Active

Irregular Verb   *(Week 9, p. 51)*

	SINGULAR	PLURAL		SINGULAR	PLURAL
1ST	possum	possumus		I am able	we are able
2ND	potes	potestis		you are able	you all are able
3RD	potest	possunt		he/she/it is able	they are able

NOUNS

First Declension Noun Endings

(Week 10, p. 57)

	SINGULAR	PLURAL		SINGULAR	PLURAL
NOM.	-a	-ae		a, the *noun*	the *nouns*
GEN.	-ae	-ārum		of the *noun*, the *noun's*	of the *nouns*, the *nouns'*
DAT.	-ae	-īs		to, for the *noun*	to, for the *nouns*
ACC.	-am	-ās		the *noun*	the *nouns*
ABL.	-ā	-īs		by, with, from the *noun*	by, with, from the *nouns*

Second Declension Noun Endings

(Week 11, p. 63)

	SINGULAR	PLURAL		SINGULAR	PLURAL
NOM.	-us	-ī		a, the *noun*	the *nouns*
GEN.	-ī	-ōrum		of the *noun*, the *noun's*	of the *nouns*, the *nouns'*
DAT.	-ō	-īs		to, for the *noun*	to, for the *nouns*
ACC.	-um	-ōs		the *noun*	the *nouns*
ABL.	-ō	-īs		by, with, from the *noun*	by, with, from the *nouns*

Second Declension Neuter Noun Endings

(Week 20, p. 113)

	SINGULAR	PLURAL		SINGULAR	PLURAL
NOM.	-um	-a		a, the *noun*	the *nouns*
GEN.	-ī	-ōrum		of the *noun*, the *noun's*	of the *nouns*, the *nouns'*
DAT.	-ō	-īs		to, for the *noun*	to, for the *nouns*
ACC.	-um	-a		the *noun*	the *nouns*
ABL.	-ō	-īs		by, with, from the *noun*	by, with, from the *nouns*

PRONOUNS

Hic, haec, hoc: *this*
Singular Demonstrative Pronouns / Adjectives
(Week 22, p. 129)

	MASCULINE	FEMININE	NEUTER		SINGULAR
NOM.	hic	haec	hoc		this
GEN.	huius	huius	huius		of this
DAT.	huic	huic	huic		to, for this
ACC.	hunc	hanc	hoc		this
ABL.	hōc	hāc	hōc		by, with, from this

Hī, hae, haec: *these*
Plural Demonstrative Pronouns / Adjectives
(Week 23, p. 135)

	MASCULINE	FEMININE	NEUTER		PLURAL
NOM.	hī	hae	haec		these
GEN.	hōrum	hārum	hōrum		of these
DAT.	hīs	hīs	hīs		to, for these
ACC.	hōs	hās	haec		these
ABL.	hīs	hīs	hīs		by, with, from these

Ego, nōs: *I, we*
Personal Pronouns
(Week 24, p. 141)

	SINGULAR	PLURAL		SINGULAR	PLURAL
NOM.	ego	nōs		I	we
GEN.	meī	nostrum		of me, my	of us
DAT.	mihi	nōbīs		to, for me	to, for us
ACC.	mē	nōs		me	us
ABL.	mē	nōbīs		by, with, from me	by, with, from us

Tū, vōs: *you, you all*

Personal Pronouns

(Week 24, p. 142)

	SINGULAR	PLURAL		SINGULAR	PLURAL
NOM.	tū	vōs		you	you all
GEN.	tuī	vestrum		of you	of you all
DAT.	tibi	vōbīs		to, for you	to, for you all
ACC.	tē	vōs		you	you all
ABL.	tē	vōbīs		by, with, from you	by, with, from you all

Verb Chants, applied to Amō and Videō

The chants in this section follow the conjugation of amō *(1st conj.) and* videō *(2nd conj.). The notation [PV] stands for "passive voice." Conjugations without this notation are in the active voice.*

LATIN	SINGULAR			PLURAL		
	1ST	2ND	3RD	1ST	2ND	3RD
PRESENT	amō	amās	amat	amāmus	amātis	amant
FUTURE	amābō	amābis	amābit	amābimus	amābitis	amābunt
IMPERFECT	amābam	amābās	amābat	amābāmus	amābātis	amābant
PERFECT	amāvī	amāvistī	amāvit	amāvimus	amāvistis	amāvērunt
FUTURE PERFECT	amāverō	amāveris	amāverit	amāverimus	amāveritis	amāverint
PLUPERFECT	amāveram	amāverās	amāverat	amāverāmus	amāverātis	amāverant
PRESENT [PV]	amor	amāris	amātur	amāmur	amāminī	amantur
FUTURE [PV]	amābor	amāberis	amābitur	amābimur	amābiminī	amābuntur
IMPERFECT [PV]	amābar	amābāris	amābātur	amābāmur	amābāminī	amābantur

ENGLISH	SINGULAR			PLURAL		
	1ST	2ND	3RD	1ST	2ND	3RD
PRESENT	I love	you love	he/she/it loves	we love	you all love	they love
FUTURE	I will love	you will love	he/she/it will love	we will love	you all will love	they will love
IMPERFECT	I was loving	you were loving	he/she/it was loving	we were loving	you all were loving	they were loving
PERFECT	I have loved	you have loved	he/she/it has loved	we have loved	you all have loved	they have loved
FUTURE PERFECT	I will have loved	you will have loved	he/she/it will have loved	we will have loved	you all will have loved	they will have loved
PLUPERFECT	I had loved	you had loved	he/she/it had loved	we had loved	you all had loved	they had loved
PRESENT [PV]	I am loved	you are loved	he/she/it is loved	we are loved	you all are loved	they are loved
FUTURE [PV]	I will be loved	you will be loved	he/she/it will be loved	we will be loved	you all will be loved	they will be loved
IMPERFECT [PV]	I was being loved	you were being loved	he/she/it was being loved	we were being loved	you all were being loved	they were being loved

LATIN	SINGULAR			PLURAL		
	1ST	2ND	3RD	1ST	2ND	3RD
PRESENT	vide**ō**	vid**ēs**	vide**t**	vidē**mus**	vidē**tis**	vid**ent**
FUTURE	vidē**bō**	vidē**bis**	vidē**bit**	vidē**bimus**	vidē**bitis**	vidē**bunt**
IMPERFECT	vidē**bam**	vidē**bās**	vidē**bat**	vidē**bāmus**	vidē**bātis**	vidē**bant**
PERFECT	vid**ī**	vid**istī**	vid**it**	vid**imus**	vid**istis**	vid**ērunt**
FUTURE PERFECT	vid**erō**	vid**eris**	vid**erit**	vid**erimus**	vid**eritis**	vid**erint**
PLUPERFECT	vid**eram**	vid**erās**	vid**erat**	vid**erāmus**	vid**erātis**	vid**erant**
PRESENT [PV]	vidē**or**	vidē**ris**	vidē**tur**	vidē**mur**	vidē**minī**	vidē**ntur**
FUTURE [PV]	vidē**bor**	vidē**beris**	vidē**bitur**	vidē**bimur**	vidē**biminī**	vidē**buntur**
IMPERFECT [PV]	vidē**bar**	vidē**bāris**	vidē**bātur**	vidē**bāmur**	vidē**bāminī**	vidē**bantur**

ENGLISH	SINGULAR			PLURAL		
	1ST	2ND	3RD	1ST	2ND	3RD
PRESENT	I see	you see	he/she/it sees	we see	you all see	they see
FUTURE	I will see	you will see	he/she/it will see	we will see	you all will see	they will see
IMPERFECT	I was seeing	you were seeing	he/she/it was seeing	we were seeing	you all were seeing	they were seeing
PERFECT	I have seen	you have seen	he/she/it has seen	we have seen	you all have seen	they have seen
FUTURE PERFECT	I will have seen	you will have seen	he/she/it will have seen	we will have seen	you all will have seen	they will have seen
PLUPERFECT	I had seen	you had seen	he/she/it had seen	we had seen	you all had seen	they had seen
PRESENT [PV]	I am seen	you are seen	he/she/it is seen	we are seen	you all are seen	they are seen
FUTURE [PV]	I will be seen	you will be seen	he/she/it will be seen	we will be seen	you all will be seen	they will be seen
IMPERFECT [PV]	I was being seen	you were being seen	he/she/it was being seen	we were being seen	you all were being seen	they were being seen

GLOSSARY

A

ad *to, toward* (Week 12)

administrō (administrāre) *I help, manage* (1st conj., Week 5)

adulēscēns *young man* (3rd decl., Week 22)

aedificium, -ī *building* (2nd decl., Week 15)

aequus, -a, -um *level, even, calm* (Week 23)

ager, agrī *field* (2nd decl., Week 12)

agō *I do, act* (3rd conj., Week 10)

agricola, -ae *farmer* (1st decl., Week 25)

albus, -a, -um *white* (Week 25)

aliēnus, -a, -um *foreign* (Week 26)

ambulō (ambulāre) *I walk* (1st conj., Week 10)

amīcus, -ī *friend* (2nd decl., Week 2)

amō (amāre) *I love* (1st conj., Week 1)

ancora, -ae *anchor* (1st decl., Week 23)

animal *animal* (3rd decl., Week 25)

animus, -ī *mind* (2nd decl., Week 22)

annus, -ī *year* (2nd decl., Week 27)

ante *before* (Week 27)

antīquus, -a, -um *ancient* (Week 17)

apostolus, -ī *apostle* (2nd decl., Week 24)

appellō (appellāre) *I name* (1st conj., Week 22)

aqua, -ae *water* (1st decl., Week 8)

aquārius, -ī *water-carrier* (2nd decl., Week 21)

aquila, -ae *eagle* (1st decl., Week 19)

arbor *tree* (3rd decl., Week 6)

ariēs *ram* (3rd decl., Week 21)

audeō (audēre) *I dare* (2nd conj., Week 12)

audiō *I hear* (4th conj., Week 2)

augeō (augēre) *I increase* (2nd conj., Week 15)

aura, -ae *breeze* (1st decl., Week 19)

aurīga, -ae *charioteer* (1st decl., Week 21)

auris *ear* (3rd decl., Week 13)

aurōra, -ae *dawn* (1st decl., Week 21)

austrālis *southern* (Week 21)

auxilium, -ī *help, aid* (2nd decl., Week 20)

avis *bird* (3rd decl., Week 3)

avus, -ī *grandfather* (2nd decl., Week 22)

B

beātus, -a, -um *happy, blessed* (Week 22)

bellum, -ī *war* (2nd decl., Week 9)

bene *well* (Week 19)

beneficium, -ī *kindness* (2nd decl., Week 20)

Biblia Sacra *Holy Bible* (1st decl., Week 24)

bonus, -a, -um *good* (Week 4)

borēus, -a, -um *northern* (Week 21)

bracchium, -ī *arm* (2nd decl., Week 5)

C

caelum, -ī *sky* (2nd decl., Week 3)

campus, -ī *level area, athletic field* (2nd decl., Week 16)

cancer, -crī *crab* (2nd decl., Week 21)

canis *dog* (3rd decl., Week 2)

capillus, -ī *hair* (2nd decl., Week 13)

capiō *I take, capture* (3rd conj., Week 9)

captīvus, -ī *captive* (2nd decl., Week 16)

caput *head* (3rd decl., Week 1)

castellum, -ī *castle* (2nd decl., Week 9)

castra, -ōrum *camp* (2nd decl., Week 16)

censeō (censēre) *I estimate* (2nd conj., Week 26)

centum *one hundred* (indecl., Week 11)

Christus, -ī *Christ* (2nd decl., Week 24)

cibus, -ī *food* (2nd decl., Week 25)

cīvis *citizen* (3rd decl., Week 15)

clam *secretly* (Week 19)

clāmō (clāmāre) *I shout* (1st conj., Week 3)

classis *fleet (of ships)* (3rd decl., Week 23)

cōgitō (cōgitāre) *I think* (1st. conj., Week 2)

collis *hill* (3rd decl., Week 6)

colōnus, -ī *settler* (2nd decl., Week 18)

commūnicō (commūnicāre) *I share, inform* (1st conj., Week 15)

contentus, -a, -um *satisfied, content* (Week 22)

contrā *against* (Week 9)

cōpiae, -ārum *troops* (1st decl., Week 9)

cor *heart* (3rd decl., Week 13)

corōna, -ae *crown* (1st decl., Week 18)

corpus *body* (3rd decl., Week 5)

crās *tomorrow* (Week 27)

crēdō *I believe* (3rd conj., Week 24)

creō (creāre) *I create* (1st conj., Week 3)

crūs *leg* (3rd decl., Week 5)

crux *cross* (3rd decl., Week 10)

cūrō (cūrāre) *I care for* (1st conj., Week 7)

currō *I run* (3rd conj., Week 6)

D

dēbeō (dēbēre) *I owe, ought* (2nd conj., Week 10)

decem *ten* (indecl., Week 11)

dēlectō (dēlectāre) *I delight* (1st conj., Week 19)

dēleō (dēlēre) *I destroy* (2nd conj., Week 14)

dēmonstrō (dēmonstrāre) *I show* (1st conj., Week 4)

dēspērō (dēspērāre) *I despair* (1st conj., Week 7)

Deus, -ī *God* (2nd decl., Week 3)

diēs *day* (5th decl., Week 8)

difficilis *difficult* (Week 12)

digitus, -ī *finger* (2nd decl., Week 13)

dīrigō *I direct* (3rd conj., Week 4)

disciplīna, -ae *instruction, training* (1st decl., Week 22)

discipula, -ae *student (female)* (1st decl., Week 4)

discipulus, -ī *student (male)* (2nd decl., Week 4)

dō (dāre) *I give* (1st conj., Week 3)

doceō *I teach* (2nd conj., Week 4)

doleō (dolēre) *I grieve* (2nd conj., Week 13)

dominus, -ī *lord, master* (2nd decl., Week 12)

domus *house, home* (4th decl., Week 2)

dōnum, -ī *gift* (2nd decl., Week 20)

dubitō (dubitāre) *I doubt* (1st conj., Week 12)

dulcis *sweet* (Week 13)

duo *two* (Week 11)

dux *leader* (3rd decl., Week 18)

E

ecce *behold!* (Week 27)

ecclēsia, -ae *church* (1st decl., Week 24)

equus, -ī *horse* (2nd decl., Week 9)

errō (errāre) *I wander* (1st conj., Week 22)

et *and* (Week 1)

ēvangelium, -ī *good news* (2nd decl., Week 24)

ex *out of, from* (Week 8)

exerceō (exercēre) *I train, exercise* (2nd conj., Week 16)

exercitus *army* (4th decl., Week 17)

explōrō (explōrāre) *I find out, explore* (1st conj., Week 19)

exspectō (exspectāre) *I wait for* (1st conj., Week 7)

F

faciēs *face* (5th decl., Week 13)

facilis *easy* (Week 12)

faciō *I make, do* (3rd conj., Week 6)

fāma, -ae *report, reputation* (1st decl., Week 17)

famēs *hunger, famine, starvation* (3rd decl., Week 25)

familia, -ae *household* (1st decl., Week 10)

fēmina, -ae *woman* (1st decl., Week 6)

ferus, -a, -um *fierce, wild* (Week 17)

fidēs *faith* (5th decl., Week 24)

fīlia, -ae *daughter* (1st decl., Week 10)

fīlius, -ī *son* (2nd decl., Week 10)

fīnis *the end* (3rd decl., Week 27)

fleō (flēre) *I weep* (2nd conj., Week 14)

flōreō (flōrēre) *I flourish* (2nd conj., Week 19)

flūmen *river* (3rd decl., Week 3)

folium, -ī *leaf* (2nd decl., Week 20)

fortis *strong, brave* (Week 13)

forum, -ī *public square, marketplace* (2nd decl., Week 26)

fossa, -ae *ditch* (1st decl., Week 25)

frāter *brother* (3rd decl., Week 6)

G

Gallia, -ae *Gaul* (1st decl., Week 15)

geminus, -ī *twin* (2nd decl., Week 21)

gens *tribe* (3rd decl., Week 18)

Germānia, -ae *Germany* (1st decl., Week 15)

gladius, -ī *sword* (2nd decl., Week 9)

glōria, -ae *fame, glory* (1st decl., Week 10)

grātiae, -ārum *thanks* (1st decl., Week 12)

grātiās agō *thanks!* (Week 13)

H

habeō (habēre) *I have, hold* (2nd conj., Week 8)

herba, -ae *herb, plant* (1st decl., Week 19)

herī *yesterday* (Week 27)

Hispānia, -ae *Spain* (1st decl., Week 15)

hodiē *today* (Week 27)

homō *man, human being* (3rd decl., Week 10)

honestus, -a, -um *honorable* (Week 22)

hōra, -ae *hour* (1st decl., Week 27)

hortus, -ī *garden* (2nd decl., Week 25)

hostis *enemy* (3rd decl., Week 17)

I

Iesus *Jesus* (4th decl., Week 24)

ignis *fire* (3rd decl., Week 9)

imperō (imperāre) *I order* (1st conj., Week 7)

improbus, -a, -um *wicked* (Week 22)

in *in, into* (Week 5)

iniūria, -ae *injury* (1st decl., Week 17)

īnsula, -ae *island* (1st decl., Week 6)

inter *between* (Week 26)

īra, -ae *anger* (1st decl., Week 26)

Ītalia, -ae *Italy* (1st decl., Week 15)

iter *journey* (3rd decl., Week 23)

iubeō (iubēre) *I order* (2nd conj., Week 17)

iuvō (iuvāre) *I help* (1st conj., Week 15)

L

labor *work, toil* (3rd decl., Week 8)

labōrō (labōrāre) *I work* (1st conj., Week 4)

lātus, -a, -um *wide, broad* (Week 23)

laudō (laudāre) *I praise* (1st conj., Week 2)

lēgātus, -ī *lieutenant* (2nd decl., Week 17)

lēgō (lēgāre) *I appoint* (1st conj., Week 18)

leō *lion* (3rd decl., Week 21)

lex *law* (3rd decl., Week 10)

liber, librī *book* (2nd decl., Week 4)

līberō (līberāre) *I set free* (1st conj., Week 5)

lībra, -ae *pair of scales* (1st decl., Week 21)

lingua, -ae *language* (1st decl., Week 26)

longus, -a, -um *long* (Week 13)

lūdus, -ī *game, school* (2nd decl., Week 4)

lūna, -ae *moon* (1st decl., Week 3)

lupus, -ī *wolf* (2nd decl., Week 19)

lux *light* (3rd decl., Week 3)

M

magister, magistrī *teacher (male)* (2nd decl., Week 4)

magistra, -ae *teacher (female)* (1st decl., Week 4)

magnus, -a, -um *large* (Week 4)

māior *greater* (Week 21)

malus, -a, -um *bad, evil* (Week 5)

maneō (manēre) *I remain* (2nd conj., Week 15)

manus *hand* (4th decl., Week 5)

mare *sea* (3rd decl., Week 3)

māter *mother* (3rd decl., Week 2)

mediocris *ordinary* (Week 26)

mens *mind* (3rd decl., Week 13)

mensa, -ae *table* (1st decl., Week 12)

mensis *month* (3rd decl., Week 27)

mereō (merēre) *I deserve* (2nd conj., Week 15)

merīdiēs *noon* (5th decl., Week 27)

metus *fear* (4th decl., Week 9)

mīles *soldier* (3rd decl., Week 9)

mille *one thousand* (indecl., Week 11)

minor *smaller* (Week 21)

mīrus, -a, -um *strange, wonderful* (Week 26)

miser, -era, -erum *unhappy, wretched, miserable* (Week 18)

moenia *fortifications, city walls* (3rd decl., Week 16)

moneō (monēre) *I warn* (2nd conj., Week 13)

mons *mountain* (3rd decl., Week 3)

mors *death* (3rd decl., Week 24)

moveō (movēre) *I move* (2nd conj., Week 8)

multus, -a, -um *much, many* (Week 27)

mūrus, -ī *wall* (2nd decl., Week 16)

mūtō (mūtāre) *I change* (1st conj., Week 5)

N

nauta, -ae *sailor* (1st decl., Week 8)

nāvigō (nāvigāre) *I sail* (1st conj., Week 8)

nāvis *ship* (3rd decl., Week 8)

necō (necāre) *I kill* (1st conj., Week 14)

negō (negāre) *I deny* (1st conj., Week 18)

nihil *nothing* (indecl., Week 3)

nimbus, -ī *cloud* (2nd decl., Week 19)

nō (nāre) *I swim* (1st conj., Week 23)

noceō (nocēre) *I harm* (2nd conj., Week 17)

nomen *name* (3rd decl., Week 6)

nōn *not* (Week 18)

novem *nine* (indecl., Week 11)

novus, -a, -um *new* (Week 5)

nox *night* (3rd decl., Week 8)

numerus, -ī *number* (2nd decl., Week 11)

nunc *now* (Week 10)

nuntius, -ī *message, messenger* (2nd decl., Week 17)

O

occultō (occultāre) *I hide* (1st conj., Week 19)

occupō (occupāre) *I seize* (1st conj., Week 14)

octō *eight* (indecl., Week 11)

oculus, -ī *eye* (2nd decl., Week 5)

oppidum, -ī *town* (2nd decl., Week 15)

oppugnō (oppugnāre) *I attack* (1st conj., Week 9)

ōra, -ae *shore* (1st decl., Week 23)

ōrō (ōrāre) *I pray, speak* (1st conj., Week 5)

ōs *mouth* (3rd decl., Week 5)

P

pābulum, -ī *fodder, food for animals* (2nd decl., Week 20)

pāreō (pārēre) *I obey* (2nd conj., Week 13)

parō (parāre) *I prepare* (1st conj., Week 16)

parvus, -a, -um *little* (Week 4)

pastor *shepherd* (3rd decl., Week 25)

pater *father* (3rd decl., Week 2)

patientia, -ae *patience* (1st decl., Week 22)

patria, -ae *native land* (1st decl., Week 8)

paucī, -ae, -a *few* (Week 11)

pax *peace* (3rd decl., Week 24)

pecūnia, -ae *money* (1st decl., Week 11)

perīculum, -ī *danger* (2nd decl., Week 9)

perturbō (perturbāre) *I confuse* (1st conj., Week 17)

pēs *foot* (3rd decl., Week 5)

pīlum, -ī *javelin* (2nd decl., Week 20)

piscis *fish* (3rd decl., Week 21)

placeō (placēre) *I please* (2nd conj., Week 22)

poena, -ae *penalty, punishment* (1st decl., Week 24)

pōnō *I put, place* (3rd conj., Week 12)

pons *bridge* (3rd decl., Week 23)

populus, -ī *people, nation* (2nd decl., Week 18)

porta, -ae *door, gate* (1st decl., Week 12)

portō (portāre) *I carry* (1st conj., Week 4)

portus *harbor* (4th decl., Week 23)

possum *I am able* (irreg., Week 9)

post *after* (Week 27)

postulō (postulāre) *I demand* (1st conj., Week 26)

potens *powerful* (Week 18)

praeda, -ae *plunder, booty* (1st decl., Week 16)

praedīcō *I proclaim* (3rd conj., Week 24)

praefectus, -ī *officer* (2nd decl., Week 16)

praemium, -ī *reward* (2nd decl., Week 20)

prīmus, -a, -um *first* (Week 27)

princeps *chief* (3rd decl., Week 16)

probō (probāre) *I approve* (1st conj., Week 18)

prohibeō (prohibēre) *I prevent* (2nd conj., Week 18)

prope *near* (Week 23)

puella, -ae *girl* (1st decl., Week 2)

puer, puerī *boy* (2nd decl., Week 2)

pugna, -ae *fight* (1st decl., Week 17)

pulvis *dirt, dust, powder* (3rd decl., Week 25)

putō (putāre) *I think* (1st conj., Week 16)

Q

quattuor *four* (indecl., Week 11)

quinque *five* (indecl., Week 11)

R

recitō (recitāre) *I read aloud* (1st conj., Week 22)

recuperō (recuperāre) *I recover* (1st conj., Week 16)

recūsō (recūsāre) *I refuse* (1st conj., Week 18)

rēgīna, -ae *queen* (1st decl., Week 18)

regnum, -ī *kingdom* (2nd decl., Week 20)

regō *I rule* (3rd conj., Week 10)

rēmus, -ī *oar* (2nd decl., Week 23)

rēs *thing* (5th decl., Week 26)

respondeō (respondēre) *I answer* (2nd conj., Week 14)

rēx *king* (3rd decl., Week 10)

rīdeō (rīdēre) *I laugh* (2nd conj., Week 10)

rīpa, -ae *bank (of a creek or river)* (1st decl., Week 19)

rogō (rogāre) *I ask* (1st conj., Week 22)

Rōma, -ae *Rome* (1st decl., Week 15)

S

sacculus, -ī *little bag* (2nd decl., Week 26)

saepe *often* (Week 8)

sagitta, -ae *arrow* (1st decl., Week 17)

sagittārius, -ī *archer* (2nd decl., Week 21)

salvē *Good day! (Be well)* (Week 2)

satis *enough* (Week 19)

saxum, -ī *rock* (2nd decl., Week 20)

sciō *I know* (4th conj., Week 27)

scorpius, -ī *scorpion* (2nd decl., Week 21)

scrībō *I write* (3rd conj., Week 6)

scūtum, -ī *shield* (2nd decl., Week 20)

sedeō (sedēre) *I sit* (2nd conj., Week 8)

sēmen *seed* (3rd decl., Week 25)

semper *always* (Week 4)

sententia, -ae *opinion* (1st decl., Week 26)

septem *seven* (indecl., Week 11)

serō *I sow, plant* (3rd conj., Week 25)

servō (servāre) *I save* (1st conj., Week 10)

servus, -ī *slave* (2nd decl., Week 12)

sex *six* (indecl., Week 11)

sīca, -ae *dagger* (1st decl., Week 17)

signum, -ī *sign* (2nd decl., Week 20)

silentium, -ī *silence* (2nd decl., Week 20)

silva, -ae *forest* (1st decl., Week 6)

simulō (simulāre) *I pretend* (1st conj., Week 7)

socius, -ī *partner, associate* (2nd decl., Week 18)

sōl *sun* (3rd decl., Week 3)

solum, -ī *floor, ground* (2nd decl., Week 12)

soror *sister* (3rd decl., Week 6)

spectō (spectāre) *I look at, watch* (1st conj., Week 13)

spēlunca, -ae *cave* (1st decl., Week 19)

spērō (spērāre) *I hope* (1st conj., Week 6)

spēs *hope* (5th decl., Week 24)

stabulum, -ī *stall, stable* (2nd decl., Week 25)

stagnum, -ī *pond* (2nd decl., Week 20)

stella, -ae *star* (1st decl., Week 3)

stō (stāre) *I stand* (1st conj., Week 12)

stultus, -a, -um *foolish* (Week 22)

sub *below* (Week 6)

sum *I am* (irreg., Week 2)

superō (superāre) *I conquer* (1st conj., Week 16)

suprā *above* (Week 6)

T

tardō (tardāre) *I delay* (1st conj., Week 5)

taurus, -ī *bull* (2nd decl., Week 19)

tēlum, -ī *weapon* (2nd decl., Week 20)

tempestās *weather, storm* (3rd decl., Week 23)

tempus *time* (3rd decl., Week 27)

teneō (tenēre) *I hold, possess* (2nd conj., Week 13)

terra, -ae *earth, land* (1st decl., Week 3)

terreō (terrēre) *I frighten* (2nd conj., Week 9)

timeō (timēre) *I fear* (2nd conj., Week 9)

toga, -ae *toga* (1st decl., Week 26)

trēs *three* (Week 11)

triumphus, -ī *triumph* (2nd decl., Week 17)

U

unda, -ae *wave* (1st decl., Week 23)

ūnus, -a, -um *one* (Week 11)

urbs *city* (3rd decl., Week 15)

ursa, -ae *or* **ursus, -ī** *bear* (1st decl. *or* 2nd decl., Week 21)

V

valē *Goodbye! (Be well)* (Week 2)

valeō (valēre) *I am well* (2nd conj., Week 8)

vēlum, -ī *sail* (2nd decl., Week 23)

ventus, -ī *wind* (2nd decl., Week 23)

verbum, -ī *word* (2nd decl., Week 20)

vērus, -a, -um *true* (Week 24)

vesper *evening, evening star* (3rd decl., Week 8)

via, -ae *road, way* (1st decl., Week 15)

vīcus, -ī *village* (2nd decl., Week 16)

videō (vidēre) *I see* (2nd conj., Week 8)

villa, -ae *farmhouse, country house* (1st decl., Week 25)

vincō *I conquer* (3rd conj., Week 9)

vīnum, -ī *wine* (2nd decl., Week 25)

vir, virī *man* (2nd decl., Week 2)

virgō *maiden* (3rd decl., Week 21)

vīta, -ae *life* (1st decl., Week 10)

vītō (vītāre) *I avoid* (1st conj., Week 26)

vīvō *I live* (3rd conj., Week 2)

vīvus, -a, -um *living* (Week 24)

vocō (vocāre) *I call* (1st conj., Week 6)

volō (volāre) *I fly* (1st conj., Week 12)

vox *voice* (3rd decl., Week 26)

vulnerō (vulnerāre) *I wound* (1st conj., Week 25)

vulnus *wound* (3rd decl., Week 16)

SOURCES AND HELPS

Brunel, Donald J., Jr. *Basic Latin Vocabulary.* Oxford: American Classical League, 1909. In the later stages of developing the curriculum, this was my basic source for choosing and defining vocabulary.

Buehner, William J. and Ambrose, John W. *Introduction to Preparatory Latin,* Book I, 2nd ed. Wellesley Hills: Independent School Press, 1977.

Ehrlich, Eugene. *Amo, Amas, Amat, and More.* New York: Harper and Row, 1985.

Morris, William, ed. *American Heritage Dictionary of the English Language,* New College Edition. Boston: Houghton Mifflin, 1976. This was my basic reference English dictionary and one I would recommend for the teaching of Latin. My main use for it was in confirming and defining derivatives.

Schaeffer, Rudolph F. *Latin English Derivative Dictionary,* edited by W.C. Carr. Oxford: American Classical League, 1960.

Simpson, D.P. *Cassell's Latin and English Dictionary.* New York: Macmillan Publishing, 1987. This is my most commonly used Latin dictionary, as well as the one the students used in their work.

Weber, Robertus, ed. *Biblia Sacra Vulgata.* Stuttgart: Wurttembergische Bibelanstalt, 1975. I used this and perhaps other versions for Scripture quotations.

Wheelock, Frederic M. *Latin: An Introductory Course Based on Ancient Authors,* 6th ed. revised. New York: Harper and Row, 2005. I depended upon this for Latin grammar and I would recommend it for teachers of Latin who need more of a Latin background.